ON the RIO GRANDE

Stories From My Life On the Border

About This Book

Joe Lewels' stories of his life growing up in far West Texas are fascinating and hilarious. His cliff-hanging exploits on and across the border shed light on the fact that El Paso/Juárez are worlds apart from the rest of Texas.

This chatty memoir is funny, insightful and, at times, heart-rending. I particularly liked his stories about his service as an army pilot in Vietnam. It's a genuine page turner. I couldn't put it down.

—**Ruth Taber, columnist,** *El Paso Inc. Magazine*

Lewels' tales of a young Mexican-American coming of age on the border are riveting. Sometimes they are zany and at other times heart breaking. He writes with great clarity and wit. His conversational style makes you feel he is speaking directly to you.

It is a much needed book about the history of the border as seen through the eyes of a kid trying desperately to assimilate into American society. The book sheds light on an area of the country that is wildly misunderstood. I highly recommend it.

—**Robert Diaz, President
El Paso County Historical Society**

What an education on the lives of people growing up on the border! Unforgettable!

—**Phyllis Galde, Publisher
Galde Press, Inc.**

On the Rio Grande

Stories From My Life On the Border

By Joe Lewels

Galde Press, Inc
www.galdepress.com

On the Rio Grande
© Copyright 2018 by Joe Lewels
All rights reserved.
Printed in the United States of America
All rights reserved. This is a work of nonfiction. No part of this work may be copied or reproduced in any way without prior permission from publisher.

First Edition, First Printing

About the Cover

This exaggerated caricature depicting the international border crossing over the Rio Grande River between El Paso, Texas and Ciudad Juárez, Mexico is reminiscent of a time when Juárez was a tourist destination, offering fine dining, exotic cabarets, numerous strip clubs, back-street brothels and even quickie divorces. The city was the night-time playground for El Pasoans, who imbibed alcohol freely while El Paso and the rest of Texas remained dry. All of this changed in more recent years when the drug wars brought unprecedented violence to El Paso's sister city, and many of the favorite establishments were burned to the ground or simply closed their doors. Its days as a mecca for American tourists may never return, but this author wishes they would. It was a unique time and a unique place where two cultures blended peacefully, and crossing the Rio Grande was a simple, daily affair.

Cover art: Patricia Stockmeyer.

Dedications and Acknowledgements

This book is dedicated to my wife, Hilda Stockmeyer Lewels; to my children, Christopher John Lewels and Marisa Gabriel Lewels Marocco (and her husband Daniel); and to my grandchildren, Paul and Benjamin Marocco. I love you all dearly. It is also dedicated to the memory of my son, Nicholas Joseph Lewels (1975-2003), and to all the refugees and immigrants around the world who are literally dying to come to America in search of safety, jobs, peace and tranquility. May God bless you and have mercy on you.

I am greatly appreciative of the wise and useful comments and corrections to my manuscript made by the following: Hilda Lewels, John Parkin, Ruth Taber, Robert Diaz and Phyllis Galde. I also wish to thank Joe Gomez for taking the time to describe to me his experiences of his life on the border. Finally, I wish to thank the officers of the El Paso County Historical Society, particularly Robert Diaz, for assisting me with my research and for giving me permission to use some of the photos from their archives. The society can be found on the internet at: www.elpasohistory.com, and the offices are located at 603 W. Yandell Dr. in El Paso's historic Sunset Heights.

ON the RIO GRANDE

Contents

Preface		ix
Chapter *Uno*	1. My *Abuelita*, the Saint	1
Chapter *Dos*	2. The Most Famous Kid in School	15
Chapter *Tres*	3. Being Dopey	31
Chapter *Cuatro*	4. Growing up Kind of Mexicany	41
Chapter *Cinco*	5. The Other Francisco	55
Chapter *Seis*	6: The Poor Mexican	65
Chapter *Siete*	7. *Abuelito's* Secret	71
Chapter *Ocho*	8. El Paso Girls are Stupid	81
Chapter *Nueve*	9. Getting Cool	93
Chapter *Diez*	10. California Dreamin'	107
Chapter *Once*	11. Old Gringo	113
Chapter *Doce*	12. Flying Solo	123
Chapter *Trece*	13. Georgia Storm	135
Chapter *Catorce*	14. One Taco Short	149
Chapter *Quince*	15. Getting Smart the Hard Way	159
Chapter *Diez y Sies*	16. Gaming the System	167
Chapter *Diez y Siet e*	17. Dumb Luck?	179
Chapter *Diez y Ocho*	18. The Hole	187
Chapter *Diez y Nueve*	19. What the Heck is *Tet*?	197
Chapter *Veinte*	20. Losing My Cool	207
Chapter *Veinte y Uno*	21. Ghosts and Other Weirdness	223
Chapter *Viente y Dos*	22. Who's in Charge Here?	233
References		243

ON the RIO GRANDE

Preface

This is the story of a kid who grew up on the Mexican border, the grandchild of Mexican refugees who arrived in El Paso, Texas in 1915.

Their horse-drawn wagon carried the family of six more than 1000 miles in a roundabout route from a small village in the northern state of Chihuahua, across the great Chihuahuan desert, to the safety of the United States. They left hurriedly with little more than the clothes on their backs in the middle of the night.

It was the violence wrought by the Mexican Revolution (1910-1920) that forced them to seek, what they believed would be, temporary shelter on the border. However, the bloody war that ultimately took 1.4 million lives lasted much longer than anyone expected. By the time it was over, they had settled in, gotten comfortable, and stayed.

That's why I was born only a few blocks from the Rio Grande River, which marks the international boundary in El Paso, and why I had to find a way to fit into American society at the price of giving up much of my cultural heritage, particularly the Spanish language, which was the language we spoke at home when I was a kid.

As a child I had no way of knowing that my hometown of El Paso was unlike any other place in America. Its uniqueness has to do with its geographical location in a valley that cuts through the Rocky Mountains and creates a pass to the north—a trail followed by the Spanish Conquistadors who named the place "El Paso Del Norte," meaning "The Pass of the North."

This fortuitous quirk of nature has made it the largest city in the United States that lies squarely on the U.S.-Mexico border, giving it a flavor all its own. El Paso and its sister city, Ciudad Juárez, Mexico, which lies on the other side of the now mostly-dry riverbed, are home to nearly two million residents, with the city of Juárez accounting for 1.2 million.

Geographically, El Paso lies in the far west corner of Texas, wedged between Old Mexico and New Mexico. Because the city is perched in the high desert (about 3,700 ft. of altitude), it enjoys an enviable climate—relatively warm winters with cool summer nights and very low humidity. El Pasoans are far removed from the dangers of hurricanes, tornadoes and earthquakes that plague other parts of the country, but they do put up with some mighty dust storms, which routinely arrive in the spring.

Although El Paso is a major port of entry and its population is about 760,000, many who visit for the first time are surprised to see that the streets are paved and that cowboys are not hitching their horses to posts in front of saloons like they do in the movies. They are disappointed to see that people don't wear cowboy hats or speak with a Texas drawl. Fortunately, there are no quick-draw gunfights in the streets of downtown, as there were in the city's colorful past of years gone by.

The fact is that in spite of their sometimes tumultuous pasts, the cities of El Paso and Juárez have, for the most part, lived in a state of peaceful coexistence and travel between the two has been easy and uneventful. All this began to change in the late 1990s as the drug war between the various cartels in Mexico became a violent nightmare that threatened to spill over into the U.S. Then, the terror attacks of 9/11 caused the department of Homeland Security to tighten the restrictions for entry into this country, for both Mexican and U.S. citizens alike. Long lines at the busy ports of entry routinely caused delays of more than an hour due to the increased vigilance of the customs officials.

Where there were once popular restaurants, bars and shopping areas in Juárez, there became a near ghost town of burned-out store fronts and streets littered daily with bodies, the result of mass shootings. In spite of this, the city of Juárez has, in recent years, experienced diminished violence and commerce between the two cities is robust.

Amazingly, the city of El Paso remains peaceful, safe, and a pleasurable place to live, even with the many thousands of immigrants fleeing the cartel violence in Mexico and rushing to live in the U.S., just as what happened during the Revolution. Today, El Paso's population is nearly 80 percent Latino, and Spanish is spoken as commonly as is English. A border fence, electronic monitoring and enhanced Border Patrol vigilance have helped to keep El Paso's crime rate and illegal border crossings relatively low, but they have also had a dramatic impact on casual visits by El Pasoans and tourists to what was once our primary tourist attraction—the Juárez nightlife.

During the 1940s, 1950s and 1960s, the timeframe when I was growing up, going to Juárez for lunch, dinner or late night entertainment was easy—a daily affair. No passport or identification was needed for Americans to move back and forth across the Rio Grande River. The City of Juárez was anxious to receive the tourist dollars and, therefore, did not bother Americans by checking for contraband. On the return, the U.S. Customs officials were content if the traveler simply uttered the words, "U.S. Citizen," and looked like an American. There was no I.D. required, except for Mexican citizens, who were required to show their passports or their "green" card, which allowed them to work or shop in El Paso.

Needless to say, Juárez was especially fascinating for teenagers and college students who could cross the bridge with ease and enjoy the freedom of being treated like an adult at the many bars, cabarets and strip clubs. Growing up in El Paso was like no other place in America. It was a unique place and a unique time, and I don't think it will ever be the same again, although I wish it would.

One of El Paso's most historic areas existed since the late 1890s when wealthy Anglo and Mexican families built majestic homes on the foothills of the cactus-strewn Mount Franklin, which overlooks the downtown area. Even the infamous Pancho Villa is rumored to have resided there in the early part of the 1900s. This area, known as Sunset Heights, became the home of some of the wealthier refugees who fled the violence in Mexico's most northern, and largest state of Chihuahua, which includes the city of Juárez. Below the beautiful mansions there were smaller homes and apartment buildings that sprang up as more and more refugees arrived. Many of those who lived there, closer to the Rio Grande River, arrived with very little, having had to leave their land, homes, and businesses behind. That is where my family lived when I was born, and that is where my story begins. It is the story of two Mexican immigrant families who found refuge in Sunset Heights, and who stayed to raise their families and to become proud Americans.

As it is with most kids, I had only a vague awareness of my family's history and the hardships they endured as the violence and horrors of the Mexican Revolution bore down upon them in 1910. I didn't even know my real name, or that my ancestry was part Spanish and German. Because so much of my family's story was never talked about, I didn't understand that we Mexicans were any different than anyone else. But that changed when I entered the public school system, which did not allow Spanish to be spoken. I found out I was going to have to learn to speak proper English, and I would somehow have to blend into the predominately Anglo schools I attended. In short, there was a lot to learn about our new country and about my family's many secrets. I was going to have to start getting smart if I was going to make it in America, and "getting smart" also meant discovering who I was and how I fit into the bigger picture. It is a journey of self-discovery that continues to this very day.

As you will see, growing up on the border and living in two cultures, simultaneously, has its difficulties. For most of my life I tried to blend into Anglo culture only to discover that, in some cases, I wasn't considered by some to be Anglo enough. Later in life, I discovered that I wasn't Mexican enough to please others. My identity seemed to lie somewhere in the middle: not quite Mexican and not quite Anglo-American. That is why I coined the term "Mexicany" to describe the state of existence that so many Hispanics find themselves in today.

Perhaps my story will help some people to see that Mexican immigrants aren't as bad as they have been made out to be by those who feel threatened by the changing face of our nation. *On the Rio Grande* is the story of a boy who, like many others then and now, grew up in two cultures, with one foot in America and the other in Mexico. It is about a family that was proud of its Mexican roots, but who had to figure out how to blend into American society. You will see that it wasn't as easy as you might think. At times our efforts to assimilate were, unintentionally, hilarious and at other times, pathetic. I invite you to meet the cast of characters who influenced my life—my family, my friends, my teachers and my mentors. I present them as they were—the good, the not-so-good, the zany, and those with good intentions gone awry.

Now having said that, I'm going to make myself a good, old-fashioned, American hamburger; I am going to spread some guacamole and salsa on it, and I'll wash it down with a cold Mexican beer. As I do this, I will offer you a toast commonly heard on the border: "*Salud, amor y pesetas, y el tiempo para gastarlos*," which means: "health, love and money and the time to enjoy them."

— Joe Lewels, 2018

My *abuelita* (little grandmother) Aurora

1

Chapter *Uno*

My *Abuelita*, the Saint

I will always think of my sweet, loving, Mexican *abuelita* (Spanish for little grandmother) as a saint, even if she did try to kill me with a butcher knife when I was only four. I know, I know; it's a conundrum. How can my grandmother be considered a saint if she tried to kill me when I was just a kid? Well, let me try to explain.

To help you understand how such a terrible thing could have happened, I'll have to take you back to the year 1948 in El Paso, Texas when my parents, my older sister, Helen, and I lived on the third-floor of the Faywood Apartments, within view of the Rio Grande River.

It was what you might charitably call an efficiency apartment, with no bathroom, only a kitchen and a family room. All tenants on the third floor shared a common, dirty bathroom, and the ice man had to carry huge blocks of ice up the stairs to keep our ice boxes cool. My sister says I used to drop bread crumbs on the floor from my high chair and say, *"para las cucarachas"* (for the cockroaches) when I was but a toddler.

The 30-year-old building was one step above a tenement. I wouldn't say it was sleazy; it was just old and a bit dirty. We lived, just barely, on the U.S. side of the Rio Grande River in a neighborhood with the glamorous-sounding name of "Sunset Heights" (kind of like Beverly Hills, just more Mexicany), an enclave of mostly Mexican immigrants, many of whom had arrived during the Mexican Revolution (1910-1920).

One floor below lived my *abuelito* and *abuelita*, whose two-bedroom, one-bath apartment seemed awesomely luxurious to me. We spent a lot of time downstairs, particularly at bath time.

The Faywood Apartments occupied an old, red-brick building that was constructed in 1918 to help house the hordes of refugees fleeing the violence of the revolution, which gravely affected the lives of those living in the northern state of Chihuahua, where much of the fighting was centered. So many refugees arrived in those years that the population of the city grew from 40,000 to 60,000 between the years 1910-1915, and they just kept coming, poor and rich alike. (My mother's family was from the little town of Jiménez (pronounced he-MEN-ez) in the southern part of the state of Chihuahua, while my father's father was from Mazatlán, Sinaloa and his wife, Carmen, was from the State of Sonora, across the border from Arizona.)

Sunset Heights had become a sanctuary for middle and upper class Mexican families who ran for their lives, leaving their homes and personal effects behind. They found jobs and settled into life in America the best they could. Even though my family was considered to be upper-middle class in Mexico, they arrived in the U.S. as decidedly lower-middle class, as a result of the loss of their lands and businesses back home. Upon their arrival, they huddled on the south side of town, near the international bridge, in an area called "little Chihuahua" or *Chihuahuita*, until they could afford to move up to Sunset Heights. Many ultimately returned to Mexico after the danger passed. However, most of those who stayed became resident aliens and their children and grandchildren became U.S. citizens. Each new generation became more and more American and less Mexican.

As their English improved and as they assimilated into American culture, they became what I call "Mexicany," living in two cultures simultaneously. That was what it was like to live in Sunset Heights when I was a kid. It was a place where both English and Spanish were spoken, where Mexican and American holidays were celebrated, and where many found their mates and married at the Holy Family Catholic Church (or in Spanish, *La Sagrada Familia*), as my parents had in 1938. It could be said that Sunset Heights was a desperate attempt by Mexican immigrants to replicate the lives they had in Mexico, but, as the years passed, it became a birthing place for new American citizens.

My mother's parents, Vicente and Aurora Cisneros, were young, in their twenties, but already with two small children, when they fled the terror wrought by the infamous revolutionary, Francisco (Pancho) Villa in 1914. My grandmother's father, Carlos Muñoz Gutiérrez, and her younger brother, Eduardo, accompanied them as they made for the border to seek refuge, and to make a new life for themselves in a new land, where they would have to learn a new language, new customs and, somehow, find new employment. Upon arrival, my great-grandfather, Carlos, used the little money he had to open a small grocery store at 625 South El Paso Street, and the whole family lived in a small room in the back.

From then on the family rented apartments or small homes, first in *Chihuahuita* and then in Sunset Heights. Their expectation was to return to their beloved Mexico to reclaim the land and possessions they lost as soon as things calmed down, so they never bought a home. Or, it might have been that the trauma of being uprooted violently from their homes in Mexico caused them to fear such a thing could happen once again, even in the U.S. In any case, by the time my mother and father married in 1938, the family lived in a small house on the corner of Missouri and Los Angeles streets in Sunset Heights only a few blocks from the Holy Family Catholic Church and across the street from the iconic Sunset Grocery, which still stands today in 2018.

Probably the best thing about the Faywood Apartments was that they

Wedding party photo taken in front of family home on the corner of Missouri and Los Angeles streets in Sunset Heights (12-30-1938). In the background is the iconic Sunset Grocery. Left to right: "Joe" Lewels, Aurora Cisneros (*abuelita* in the background), Aurora Lewels and Vicente Cisneros (*abuelito*). Sunset Heights was the first planned residential development in El Paso-1885.

had balconies facing the Rio Grande River and the outskirts of the city of Ciudad Juárez, Mexico. On hot summer nights we would all sit on the balcony eating watermelon and watching the goings-on, just beyond the train tracks and across the river. In those days that part of Juárez had no electricity, no paved streets and, for all I know, no running water. It was a hodge-podge of adobe huts with corrugated metal roofs, held together with baling wire.

As the sun was setting, the people of Juárez would light their kerosene lamps, build their campfires and start cooking their evening meals. The smoke and dust wafted up into the dry desert air, casting a red glow in the darkening sky and my grandfather, who had left his heart in Mexico and always missed the old days, would often tell us stories, often a bit bawdy and always with a funny ending. Here is one of my favorite jokes that my *abuelito* told:

"There was a German, a Frenchman and a Mexican who were walking down a path when they saw a skunk scamper into a large bush. The three immediately made a wager as to who could last the longest in the bush with the skunk. The German went first. He lasted five minutes and came out gagging and vomiting. The Frenchman lasted ten minutes before he came out gagging and vomiting. Then the Mexican went in. Fifteen minutes went by, then 20 minutes. The others began to think he must have died or passed out, but then, suddenly, the skunk ran out of the brush, staggering, gagging and vomiting. Behind him came the Mexican, with a big smile on his face and carrying his shoes in one hand." (It was much funnier in Spanish.)

It really made me laugh, even though I now realize that the joke is very racist. Was my grandfather a racist? I don't think so. He just had a very good sense of Mexican humor, the kind that is very self-deprecating and ever-aware of the stereotypes that others have of Mexicans. I think it is okay for people to tell racist jokes about those of their own kind. This is done all the time. But when others tell the jokes it is often done in a mean spirited and hurtful way. For better or worse (mostly worse) racism seems to be a natural aspect of the human condition and cultural differences such as language,

The iconic Sunset Grocery built in 1913 was a grocery on the first floor and apartments above. Today (2018) the sign remains and the apartments are occupied, but the grocery closed many years ago.

skin color and socio-economic status play a large part in that.

In spite of the hardships they had endured, my grandparents were big jokers and they loved to laugh as they told their many stories about Mexican politics, Mexican idiosyncrasies and poor, downtrodden Mexicans, who always got the short end of the stick. My grandmother, who lived in the U.S. for most of her life by the time she died, never bothered to learn English because she always believed the family would be going back to Mexico some day, and because all our neighbors were from Mexico. Spanish was the common language in Sunset Heights, just as it is today. She was proud that she had only learned five expressions in English during all those years and she would happily recite them for anyone who asked, or didn't ask. They were: "Hello. Come in. Sit down. Shut-up. Goodbye." That would always elicit a good laugh. That was one of her best jokes.

Anyway, you get the idea. We were poor, but not as poor as those folks who lived on the other side of the river. We had electricity, paved roads and food on our tables, and if we ever started feeling sorry for ourselves, all we had to do was look out the window to see a constant reminder of how grateful we should be for the little we had.

Yes, we were fortunate, but for a little boy who craved to play outdoors, the Faywood Apartments were not ideal. The building sat at 701½ West Main Street on the corner of Main St. and Los Angeles St. (We never found the other half of the building and its whereabouts remains a mystery to this day.) To my dismay, the building was torn down in the early 1960s to make way for Interstate 10, which now runs right over the old site. If they had waited a couple of more years, the building would probably have fallen down on its own, thereby saving the taxpayers a lot of money. The building was only a block away from the old Sunset Grocery, and across the street from the old Shanghai Grocery, which was owned and operated by a Chinese family, the Yees. Because their English was no better than their Spanish, we often enjoyed authentic Chinese-Mexican cuisine.

There was a sidewalk in front of the apartments, upon which I was permitted to play, and then there was Main Street, and down a hill were the train yards and the train depot. And then, a little further down was the river, which claimed many lives each year due to the dangerous eddies that would pull swimmers down into the muddy water, never to be seen again. There was nothing to prevent a child from wandering down to see the trains, which were an unending object of amazement and delight for this little boy. Inevitably, I would find myself drawn to the trains as if their immense size created their own gravity field, pulling me away from the safety of the apartment, down, down to the tracks. Oh, I knew I wasn't supposed to be there. I had been lectured many times about the dangers and about the boogey man who would stuff a kid in his duffel bag and carry him away, but they couldn't watch me all the time and, besides, it wasn't my fault that there were bad influences in the neighborhood that lured me to the dark side.

There was a group of older kids who would take me with them to play games on, in and around the train cars. One game we played was called "Getting a Free Ride." This game consisted of seeing who could grab onto the ladder of an incoming or outgoing train, and get a free ride by lifting his feet off the ground. Once the train stopped or when it got going "scary" fast, we would let go. I still remember the thrill of it and the smell of the axle grease that permeated the air (and our clothes) when we played on the trains. Then there were times when the gang would go cat hunting in the alley behind the apartments. We would each be instructed to get a brick or a rock and then we would walk down the alley, in formation, looking for stray cats. I remember throwing rocks, but I'm not sure if we ever actually hit or killed a cat. In any case it was a thrilling experience, much like playing on the fire escape.

One game I really liked was "Sliding Down on the Poles." We would climb up to the top of the fire escape behind the building and then we would clamber under the landing at the top and slide down one of the poles to the next landing. Then we would "tightrope walk" across the narrow girder from one pole to another and slide down a different pole. When we reached the ground, we would race up to the top and start again. Come to think of it, the Faywood Apartments were a great place for a kid to play, but not so great for the parents and grandparents.

Much of the burden of watching over me fell onto the shoulders of my dear *abuelita*, who was entrusted with my care when my mother was working or shopping and my dad and *abuelito* were at work. It wasn't that I was a bad boy, I was just a very active and frustrated boy. The words "*travieso*," (mischievous) and "*malcriado*," (spoiled brat) were often used to describe me when I was a kid.

One day my grandmother saw us up on the fire escape and nearly had a heart attack. (She had a bad heart anyway). She pleaded, begged and cajoled us to come down at once, but my response was to call her names, the worst names that my little four-year-old brain could concoct: "*Caca poo poo, pee pee; caca poo poo, pee pee, abuelita. Tú eres* (you are) *caca, poo poo, pee pee abuelita! Tú eres caca, poo poo, pee pee!*" I would chant over and over.

I recall that she took the insults I was hurling at her in my most hurtful way remarkably well. Instead of getting angry, she just laughed at me. It wasn't a little giggle, but more of a big guffaw. She thought I was cute! Well, that somehow had the effect of calming me down for some reason I couldn't understand, and we came down, walking on the stairs, not sliding on poles.

Now, I know what you're thinking: "Well, no wonder your grandmother tried to kill you!" But you would be wrong. It seems that I could do worse, much worse.

What really did it; what really caused her to crack and reach for the butcher knife had more to do with the love we had for each other—a love that seemed to have no boundaries. You see, part of the problem started when I was born. It wasn't my fault that I was born a boy or that Mexican parents and grandparents treated the boys like mini gods; that's just the way it was. Throughout my life, for example, my sweet little four-foot, eleven-inch mother, truly believed I was special and this notion was accepted by the rest of the family, except by, of course, my older sister, who must have resented the fact that our mother

Aerial view of El Paso's Union Depot with train tracks next to Main St. (lower right). The Rio Grande River and Ciudad Juárez are in background. (Photo courtesy of El Paso County Historical Society).

always called me "*mi rey*" (my king), but never called her "*mi reina*" (my queen). I never thought it unusual until many years later when my wife rolled her eyes at me the first time she heard my mother say it.

"What?" I asked, not understanding her reaction.

"Your mother calls you '*mi rey*', my king?" she asked.

"Yeah," I responded. "What's wrong with that?"

She just laughed and shook her head as if she had never heard of such a thing. As it turned out, she had really never heard of such a thing, and she never let me forget it. Not wanting to offend my mother, Hilda (my wife), would wait until my mother wasn't looking and then she would mimic her by mouthing the words: "My king, oh my king," as she fluttered her eyelashes at me.

That did make me question for the first time whether it was appropriate for a mother to call her son "my king." It always seemed so perfectly normal to me. I thought about asking my mom not to say it anymore, but I knew how good it made her feel, knowing her son was a king and all. So, not having the courage to hurt her feelings, I decided to let her go on calling me her king. After all, what harm could possibly come of it?

Anyway, back to the Faywood Apartments and my life as the "*concentido*," (favorite or spoiled child) of the family. This high status, which I never sought, came with special privileges, like not being punished too severely when I was caught doing something *travieso*, but cute. So, as kids will do, I just kept pushing the envelope, as they say in the aviation business, to see just how far I could go.

What I didn't realize was that my *abuelita*, whose real name was Aurora, decided to push the envelope herself, to see how much I loved her. It turned into another little game called "Hit Me in the Face." Even though she must have known that I loved her with all my heart, she began to test me while seated at the breakfast table after my *abuelito* had gone to work and we were alone. Leaning forward, she would push her face toward me and say in a kidding way, "*Pégame, pégame*," which means "Hit me, hit me." Now as naughty as I was, I would never dream of hitting my beloved grandmother, but she persisted. Day after day she would start the game at the breakfast table and we would laugh when I wouldn't do it. Then the game progressed. She would take my little hand and place it on her cheek and plead with me, "*Pégame, pégame.*" Sometimes, just to make her laugh, I would pretend to hit her and then stop my hand just a few inches away from her face. We would really laugh at that!

Well, by now, I think you can see where this is heading. One morning I must have been having a bad day. Maybe I was just tired of playing the game, or maybe I thought she really wanted me to hit her, and in some way give her some strange kind of satisfaction. Sooooo, when she pleaded with me to hit her, I made a fist, reared back and punched the living daylights out of her.

What happened next scared the Holy-Virgin-Mother-of-God daylights out of me. I saw, for the first time ever, an anger in her eyes that I could never have conceived of in my little-child brain. It must have been an anger that had been brewing and festering for years, and it released itself in an instant. Her face contorted into a face I had never seen before, and in that split second I knew I had gone too far. I had broken the envelope and I didn't want to be around to see what would happen next.

I RAN! I was off the chair quicker than a cat with a brick on its tail and I bolted for the doorway to the bedroom. Then, just as I crossed the threshold that divided the kitchen from the bedroom, I heard a terrifying noise: THWAAAAAANG. I turned back in mid stride and saw my grandmother's huge butcher knife, which a moment ago had been lying on the kitchen table, stuck solidly in the wooden floor just behind me. It was still vibrating wildly from the force with which my sweet *abuelita* had hurled the blade, aiming for my back.

Then, I turned and ran some more. I ran, shrieking like a screaming meemee, out the living room door and up the stairs and into my mother's outstretched arms. Of course my mother didn't want to believe me, but she knew something bad had happened, so she scooped me up and marched downstairs to get to the bottom of the mystery. Fortunately for me and unfortunately for my grandmother, there was a witness. It so happened that my sister had just walked into the apartment as the whole thing unfolded and she saw (with a combination of terror and glee) the knife trembling in the floor, just a step behind me. There was no denying or sugarcoating what had happened, and there was just no explaining away the terrible thing she had done. My *abuelita* was, of course, in tears and beside herself with shame and mortification. She could barely speak. If she could have, what could she say? "Well the knife was right there on the table, so I threw it at him. You know how he is."

No, there was nothing she could say to make my mother understand. But I knew what had happened. I had finally pushed the envelope too far and she just snapped. If it had been a spoon on the table, that's what she would have thrown. It's just that the butcher knife was handy. For the record, I held no grudge against my sweet *abuelita*; I forgave her completely the moment I realized that she had missed killing me. Afterward, we made up and we continued our loving (but more respectful and cautious) relationship. After all, I had learned a very important lesson that day: Don't mess with those women from the state of Chihuahua! They are sweet on the outside, but tough as Pancho Villa on the inside.

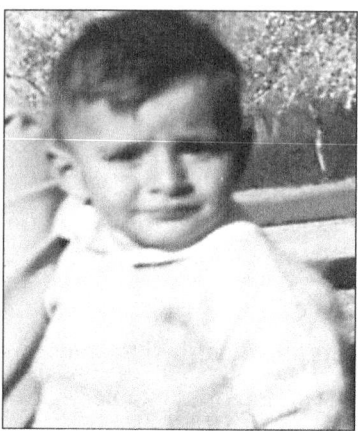

El Rey 1947—The King

My *abuelita*, Aurora Munoz de Cisneros

My *abuelito*, Vicente Cisneros Velasco

2

Chapter *Dos*

The Most Famous Kid in School

I am not certain whether my attempted murder by my grandmother was the proverbial "straw that broke the camel's back," which resulted in our moving out of the Faywood Apartments, but it probably had something to do with it.

In any case, I'm sure my grandparents were greatly relieved to be free of the burden of caring for me, and it's possible that even the neighbors chipped in to pay for new accommodations in a safer (more distant) part of town. I do remember their excitement as we drove away from the old building, my grandparents and neighbors, standing on the corner, waving handkerchiefs goodbye, as if we were leaving on a round-the-world cruise.

A new chapter in my life began when we moved to a house which was directly across the street from Mesita Elementary School, located in a fancier area of town called "Kern Place," a mostly non-Mexicany (pronounced MEX-ican-ee) neighborhood. This would be where I would attend the first grade and begin the difficult process of assimilating into American society by blending in with kids who mostly did not speak Spanish. It was made clear to me that English was the preferred language and also that I would have to shape up, if you get my drift.

I should make it clear here that my English was already pretty good because both my parents and my sister spoke English well enough. We spoke both English and Spanish at home. Both of my folks had been born in the U.S., but had dropped out of school before finishing elementary school for various reasons. My dad's English was excellent as he had worked as a reporter for the *El Paso Herald Post* for many years. My mom, however had a bit of trouble with her consonants. Instead of saying, "Would you like a 'cheese' sandwich?" she would say "Would you like a 'sheese' sandwich?" She also cleaned the floor with a "bacuum" cleaner, instead of a vacuum cleaner, and she would go "chopping," instead of shopping. As a result, no matter that she was very light skinned and had a non-Hispanic married last name, she would always be seen, on the border, as a Mexican.

In any case, I was extremely nervous on my first day in class. Not only did I have to remember not to speak Spanish, I also had to behave and to speak proper English. (You can imagine the stress I was under.) My mom and dad walked me to class on that first day to meet my teacher, Mrs. Hammond. (I remember her name quite well because forever after, my dad would refer to her as Mrs. Hammond Eggs, which would upset me, but also make me laugh.) Anyway, I was so shy that as we walked through the door that first day I hid behind my mother's skirt and wouldn't come out. Mrs. Hammond had to sweet talk me a bit to gain my confidence, and finally, she assured us that I would be just fine.

Then my parents left me, "the king," alone with a bunch of strangers. I took comfort in knowing that if things didn't work out, I could always make a mad dash for home.

What I remember most about Mrs. Hammond was that she was really, really tall, compared to my mom, so I knew immediately that I would have to try very hard not to be *travieso* or *malcriado* around her. I immediately devised a strategy that I hoped would get me through the day and the school year: I would be as inconspicuous as possible, blending in with all the strange kids as much as I could. I remember that she led me on a brief tour of the classroom and I was happy to see that there were games and activities for the kids and that, therefore, I wouldn't always be forced to sit in one place for too long, which would have been problematic for me. I also noticed that there weren't any other Mexicany-looking kids in the class, which was a good thing as I would be less likely to try to converse with anyone in the "illegal" language of Spanish.

Finally, she led me to my desk and the kids settled down. She introduced herself again, explained something about what the first grade was all about (how complicated could that have been?), and then she explained that she was going to call the roll and when our name was called, we should raise our hand and loudly say "here." I thought I would be able to handle this first task without a problem. *No problema!*

However, as I was about to learn, there was *un gran problema!* It was a problem that would propel me on the most unwanted path of making me the most famous kid in class, and maybe even the whole school! To help you understand this problem, I first have to give you a little background information, having to do with my name. As I entered the first grade, never having attended kindergarten, I had led a somewhat isolated existence. My best playmate, after we left the hooligans behind at the Faywood apartments, was my older sister, Helen, who is almost four-years older than me. Everything I knew about school and life in general, I learned from her, and when she wasn't in school, I was her slave. I looked up to her in every way and would do anything she ordered me to do. So I became an expert at playing Jacks, at choosing just the right outfits for her paper dolls, and at fashioning stylish clothes out of old socks of hers for real dolls. We did this so often, that I was acquiring quite a flair for designing ladies' fashions by the age of seven.

I would play the prince to her queen, bowing low at her command, and I would follow her around wherever she demanded me to go. I was happy to do all of this because I adored her, even if she resented me a bit for replacing

Map showing rail line from Juárez to Mexico City and the circuitous route traveled by the Cisneros/Muñoz family in 1914 during their desperate flight from Pancho Villa's death sentence. The journey in horse-drawn wagon took them from the town of Jiménez, south to Torreón, and then to Laredo, to the safety of the U.S. The last leg of the trip took them from San Antonio to El Paso.

her as the favorite in the family the moment I was born. (For the record, I still adore her.)

However, there was a day when she took my obedience too far. We were playing on the floor of the bedroom in our new house when she said, "You see this screwdriver? You see the yellow handle? Well, let's see if it lights up like a light bulb when we plug it in." I understood that when she said "we," she really meant me. As always I was obedient to her every wish and I was also curious to see if the yellow, translucent handle would light up. So, like a little dummy, I did it. I stuck the screwdriver into the electrical outlet. What do you think happens when you do this? Why not go find a screwdriver and go try this yourself? Right now.

No, I didn't think so. But, still, you may not be sure what would happen. Maybe the handle does light up. Maybe nothing happens. Maybe your hair would stand on end, making you look like Einstein. Maybe you would feel tingly all over your body. Maybe you would die. Well, you don't have to go experiment on my account, because I am about to tell you. What happened was that there was a great big BANG! Then, all the lights in the house went out and I was tossed like a rag doll all the way across the room. The handle did not light up, but sparks went flying everywhere and every fuse in the house was blown to bits.

Now aren't you glad you don't have to try this for yourself? Well, my sister was sure glad she didn't have to—at least for about a minute. That's when my parents, who had been painting a wall in our new living room, came running through the darkness (paint rollers in hand), into the bedroom where I had just about been fried. They found their way by homing in on the sound of the shrieks that were emanating from my poor little body, kind of like what Jodie Foster described in the movie, *Silence of the Lambs*, when the poor little lambs were being slaughtered. Okay, maybe I am getting a bit overly dramatic here, but I really could have been killed, once again. (As you might recall, I already had several close calls with death by this time: the butcher knife incident, the railroad trains and the fire escape, just to mention a few! Little did I know then that I was destined to have many more close calls in the years to come.) After I regained consciousness, and when our parents sorted out what had happened, I was delighted to see it was my sister's turn to get into trouble, for once.

Anyway, I have strayed somewhat from the point of the story, which is about me and my efforts to maintain as low a profile as possible in the first grade: a plan that met with spectacular failure on my first day in class. It all had to do with the fact that my parents never really explained everything to me the way one would expect parents to do.

They should have explained that Mexicans have this thing about naming their children after themselves. For example, one of my favorite cousins is named Vicente Cisneros. (Cisneros was his father's last name and thus my mother's maiden name, because they were brother and sister. The problem is that my cousin's father (my uncle) was also Vicente Cisneros as was his (our) grandfather and our great grandfather. My cousin named his son Vicente also. (For all I know this thread continues all the way back into the Middle Ages.) I think you can see the problem here, especially for anyone trying to do a genealogical study of the family.

The Mexican solution for this is to (sometimes) use a different middle name for each generation. So my cousin is Vicente Julio and his son is Vicente Carlos. That helps, because it is customary in Mexico to refer to a man by both his first name and his middle name. However, this solution is taken a bit further in Mexico. To help distinguish who is whom, individuals are also called by their mother's maiden name. So my cousin is Vicente Julio Cisneros Botello and his son is Vicente Carlos Cisneros Neuman. The result is that keeping everyone's names straight in your mind requires the use of considerable memory, which in today's technological world is something we are too lazy to use. The result is confusion. In any case, now you know why Mexicans have two last names.

Now as for me, I had always been called "Joe," just as my father had been. He was "Big Joe" and I was "Little Joe." There was another name that I would respond to, however. It was the result of another Mexican custom of giving kids nicknames. These often have to do with the person's saint's day. I know what you're thinking. This is getting too complicated. And you would be right. In Mexico, most people are Catholics and Catholics are crazy about their saints. Every day on the calendar has at least one saint attached to it. There are so many saints (thousands) that keeping up with them requires a huge institution, like say, the Vatican. And more saints are being made every year.

I am not really sure how I got my nickname, but I believe that it was my grandfather, Vicente Pio (Pius) Cisneros Velasco, who was the culprit, but my sister says it was my uncle, Lilo, (one of those cheek pinchers) who I never cared for, thus making me even angrier than before. Anyway, someone, shortly after I was born said, "Oh, he was born on the day of Saint Pompey, so we should call him "Pompeyo." And so that name stuck to me for far too long. I still doubt there is a Saint Pompey, but I don't have the energy to do the research to find out at this point in my life.

Anyway, as a kid, I was called either "Joe," "Little Joe," or "Pompeyo." Because I loved my *abuelito* dearly and he would always address me as: "*Mi amigo don Pompeyo*," I rather liked the name. (The term "don" is an honorary term used to denote respect for a person in high standing.) My grandfather and I had a special bond because we spent so much time together, as my dad was away on business so much. It was my grandfather who would take me down to the river to skip rocks across the water and watch the Mexican kids swimming on the other side. We got along famously until the day his patience wore out and he pulled down my pants, put me over his lap and spanked the hell out of me. I think the shock was worse than the actual pain. I never thought he would dare to do such a thing to "the king." I don't recall what precipitated the punishment, but as you have already seen, there is no doubt I deserved it.

Sometimes my mom or dad would shorten the name "Pompeyo" and affectionately call me "Pompis." However, when I realized this was also a term used to refer to one's butt, I decided I didn't care for that variation.

Then there were some relatives who decided it would be fun to change the name to "Pimpoyo," just to tease me. That really made me mad. But the madder I got the more they would tease me. It was a good thing I didn't have to see them very often. Sometimes nicknames stick for a long time. My wife, Hilda, was called "Tata" and my mother, Aurora, was always called "Chata" by her friends and family. My wife's sister, Patricia, is still called "Tita" by some, and our friend Carmen was called "Chikis," as a kid. Fortunately for most of them the names didn't pursue them into their adult years. I could go on and on with this, but you get the idea.

So here I was, entering the first grade, having been called "Joe," "Pompeyo," or some variation thereof all of my life and it was time for roll call on the first day. Mrs. Hammond opened her notebook and began to read the names of the kids. It went something like this:

"Jan."

"Here."

"Stevie."

"Here."

"Sandy."

"Here."

"Benny."

"Here."

And then she called a name that I was not familiar with:

"Francisco."

There was no response.

She repeated: "Francisco" a bit louder. Still no response.

At this point I remember looking around the room searching for this mysterious "Francisco" who was not responding. I noticed the other kids were also craning their necks in search of the missing kid. I thought to myself: "This is really great. There is some dumb kid who doesn't even know his name. At least I'll be smarter than one kid in this class."

And then came the bombshell. Mrs. Hammond tried once more to find the culprit, so she said again, "Francisco?" and then she added a last name: "Francisco Lewels?" she queried.

At this moment I knew I was fried (once again). The awareness that she was referring to me shot through my brain like a silver bullet, like the kind they use to kill vampires in the movies. I had no choice. I raised my hand and I simultaneously slunked down in my chair as low as I could go. I forgot to say "here." The eyes of all the kids in the class were burning holes in the back of my head, but I dared not turn to look. My plan to remain anonymous was ruined by this bolt of lightning out of the blue. "How could that have happened?" I wondered. I had no answer, but I was sure going to find out. "Just wait until I get home!" I thought to myself. "Just wait!"

I hurried home as soon as the bell rang, not wanting to stay to chat with any of my classmates (as you might imagine) and I found my mother waiting for me with a big smile. "How was your first day, *mi rey*?" She asked.

"Don't *mi rey* me!" I thought. "Why didn't you tell me my name was 'Francisco'?" I yelled, not wasting any time getting to the point.

The smile on her face was instantly replaced with one of shock. Her eyes widened and then they darted about the room as if she was going to find the answer on the ceiling or walls. Finally, all she could come up with was "I thought you knew."

"How was I supposed to know?" I responded angrily. "Nobody ever told me."

"Well," she stammered, "you were named after your father."

"His name is Joe," I countered.

"Well not exactly," she said.

"Not exactly?" I said totally buffaloed at this point.

"You see," she continued, "Your father's name is really 'Francisco Jose', so we named you 'Francisco Jose' too."

"My name is Francisco Jose?" I asked in disbelief. "I thought my name was Joe?"

"Well, 'Joe' is a nickname," she continued. "It's short for 'Jose'. You see 'Jose' is Spanish for 'Joseph' and 'Joe' is short for 'Joseph'. People have called your father 'Joe' since before you were born and we just started calling you 'Joe' too."

My mind was reeling now. I felt faint. Finally I recovered enough to ask, "What is the American name for Francisco?" I was desperately hoping for a better option.

"The American name for 'Francisco' is 'Francis', you know like Saint Francis," she answered, trying to calm me down.

"Oh no! Not 'Francis'! Not 'Francis'! That's a girl's name!!" I protested.

I was stunned beyond words by this revelation. I thought maybe I would throw up. I had to think long and hard before I could conjure up a response. Finally, I said, "I don't want to be 'Francisco', or 'Francis', I want to be 'Joe'. The teacher thinks my name is 'Francisco' and so do all the kids," I cried. My tears must have had the desired effect, because my mother's eyes lit up as if she had come up with a brilliant idea.

"Why don't we just go into the kitchen and I'll make you a sheese sandwich and a tall glass of milk?" she asked, believing that could in some way solve this horrible turn of events.

"No," I cried. I don't want a SHEESE sandwich or milk!" I retorted mockingly.

"Okay, okay calm down. Don't worry," she said. "I know exactly how we are going to fix this. I will go and talk to your teacher tomorrow morning and tell her to call you "Joe" from now on. How does that sound?"

"Okay," I said, beginning to calm down. "But you have to go with me to school and tell her before she calls the roll," I lectured.

"Yes, that's what we'll do. Don't worry, I'm sure she will understand." With the problem resolved and my blood pressure down, we went into the kitchen where my mom quickly made me a "sheese" sandwich and my "special" glass of milk, which somehow had the effect of making me quite content.

(For the record, my "special" glass of milk consisted of a glass of milk spiked with whiskey. Yes, my mother spiked my milk with whiskey, just for flavoring, because I wouldn't drink milk otherwise. This worked out quite well until one night at dinner, when my dad was home, I started banging on the table and yelling "I want my whiskey."

My father's eyes widened, and his eyebrows raised as he gave my mother a stern look. "What is he talking about?" he asked. It seems my mom had never bothered to clue my dad in to her secret solution for my dislike of milk. Well, that was the end of that! I might add that, no, I did not become an alcoholic. She didn't put that much whiskey into my milk. Just a kid-size shot.)

As it turned out, Mrs. Hammond did understand and when she called roll that morning I proudly raised my hand high and shouted out "here," for all to hear when she called out, "Joe?"

As always, I know what you're thinking: "Well that's a cute story, but it isn't enough to make you famous." And you're right. It was just enough to get the ball rolling in the right direction. You see, this brief notoriety had an interesting and unexpected effect on some of the girls in the class. I am not sure why, but I began to receive some unwanted attention from a couple of the girls. Looking back on the situation, I think maybe their motherly instincts were kicking in early. They began to, in their own way, try to console the poor little dumb Mexicany boy, trying to make him feel better. Until this happened I had not completely realized what a pitiful sight I must have been in their eyes.

One girl in particular took a shine to me and she began hanging around me like a cootie that I couldn't shake. Her name was Mary Margaret and she began to walk with me after school as far as my house. Often she would linger there, trying to keep the conversation going, but as always, I just wanted to get home, so I would bid her a hasty *adieu*. Then she started asking me to walk her home. I didn't even know where she lived, but it wasn't on my street, so I rebuffed her proposal each time by explaining that I was supposed to go straight home after school. I thought I had the situation under control, but at that young age I had no idea how devious women can be when they want something from a man. I didn't know it, but I was about to get taught a harsh and early lesson in the danger of underestimating the power of the feminine mystique.

One day after school, Mary Margaret sidled up to me, as usual, just as we were heading home and once again she asked sweetly, "Joe, will you walk me home today?" Again, I explained that I had to get home or else I would get into trouble. But this time, she pulled a box of candy Jawbreakers (my favorite) out of her pocket and said "I'll give you some of these if you will go with me." She held up the box for me to see, and the sight of the many different-colored balls inside had a mesmerizing effect.

I am not sure what kind of magic spell she put on me, but my will broke down completely, as if I had suddenly become her zombie. "Well okay," I said "I guess I can go just this one time." So off we went, skipping along in tandem as if we were off to see the Wizard, each of us with a Jawbreaker in our mouth and many more still in the box.

What happened next is not very clear now and never has been. I know we walked a few blocks, but I don't know how many. I know we shared the Jawbreakers, but I also know we never got to her house. The next vivid memory I have is that we found a house that had an inclined wall on the side, by the driveway, and we began to play a game called "Roll the Jawbreakers Down to Joe." She sat at the top of the fence and would periodically roll a Jawbreaker down to me, which I would quickly pop into my mouth.

Now given that it takes a while for a Jawbreaker to melt in one's mouth, I gauge that it took several minutes before it was time for the next roll. Now it seemed to me that it hadn't taken more than a few minutes, maybe 15 at most, before we started playing the game, and another ten minutes to get to that driveway. But it must have taken considerably longer than that because suddenly a car pulled up to the curb and an angry man rolled down his window and yelled, "Mary Margaret, you get in this car right now!" Needless to say, Mary Margaret took what was left of her Jawbreakers and was gone in an instant.

"Boy," I thought to myself, "What a mean father she has." And then I leisurely walked the two or three blocks home, expecting to see my mother's smiling face, a cheese sandwich and my favorite glass of milk waiting for me when I returned.

Well, that is not exactly how things worked out. As soon as I walked into my house I was confronted by a very angry father and a very worried mother.

"Where have you been?" my father yelled angrily.

"We have been looking everywhere for you," my mother added. "We even called the police! Everyone has been looking for you."

I couldn't understand what the commotion was all about. I had only been gone for a few minutes, as far as I was concerned, and certainly not long enough to draw so much attention. I tried to explain where I had been and about the little girl with the box of Jawbreakers and that I hadn't been gone that long, but my mother said it had been "hours." I thought that was a gross exaggeration.

As you can imagine, I was very confused, but my dad wasn't. "Go to your room! You are punished. You need to know that you are always supposed to come straight home after school, and tell your little girlfriend you're not allowed to speak to her anymore."

That last comment really burned. "She's not my girlfriend!" I shot back. "She's just a stupid girl."

Humiliated, chastised and hurt, I trudged, head hung low, into my room and shut the door. Then I threw myself on my bed, face in my pillow and pretended to cry as loud as I had ever pretended to cry before. "How could everything have gone so wrong?" I thought to myself. Only I knew how hard I had tried to be a good boy and to blend in. And now this! It was a mystery.

The next morning when I awoke I was feeling much better (having gotten all that pretend crying out of my system). I thought the worst was over and life would go on as always, but I couldn't have been more wrong.

Halfway through the first hour of the day, Mrs. Hammond announced that we had a special guest and that we should all stand when he came in. It was the principal, Mr. Meadows.

Now, I would be willing to bet that most people cannot remember the name of the principal of their school when they were in the first grade, but I can. It is a name that is burned into my memory forever. That's because Mr. Meadows was not just paying the class a casual visit. It wasn't as if he always dropped by every classroom at some point during the school year to greet the children. No, he was there this day to pass on to us a very important message. In fact, he was going around to all the classes to pass on the same message that day. "What message could that possibly be?" I wondered.

When Mr. Meadows arrived, we all stood up as ordered and Mrs. Hammond introduced him to the class. To my amazement, he proceeded to walk right up to me, stand at my side, and put his hand on my shoulder. He then announced that he had a very important message for us. The message was: "It is very important for every student to go straight home after school each day."

I am not sure if I blacked out completely or not. Perhaps my heart even stopped momentarily (which would make yet another close call with death!) I know I felt all the blood rush out of my head and I began to feel woozy. I am not exactly sure what the principal said next, but I knew my goose was cooked. It seemed to me he stayed there for at least a half hour telling the story about how little Francisco/Jose/Joe had gone missing with his little girlfriend and how worried their parents had been and how even the police had joined in the manhunt. Worse even was the fact that the story was being retold throughout the school and maybe even in other school districts! The awful reality was, that In spite of my best efforts to blend in and be inconspicuous, I had become the most famous kid in school.

The Lewels family circa 1948 in downtown El Paso. Left to right: Joe, Aurora (Chata), Helen, Joe Sr. Little brother, David would not be born until 1951.

ON the RIO GRANDE

3
Chapter *Tres*
Being "Dopey"

"Hallelujah! We're moving again!"

You can imagine my great relief when I learned we would be moving again right after the school year. Jesus himself must have been looking over me, taking pity on poor, little, dumb "Francisco". I don't think I could have taken another year of being the most famous kid in school. I would be able to start anew, with a clean slate, so to speak, at a new school where no one knew my sad history.

This time we moved clear across town to the eastside and my new school, Hillside Elementary, would be my new home-away-from home. I was in seventh heaven, anonymous once again! It was there, at Hillside School that my life was to take another amazing turn. I fell desperately in love on the first day.

My second-grade teacher, Miss Jeanne Oppenheimer (now Moye), was the most beautiful woman I had ever seen. She looked just like Snow White. I immediately fell deeply in love with her. I forgot all about being inconspicuous and I started raising my hand whenever she asked a question, even if I didn't really know the answer. This was very out of character for me, but I didn't seem to care. During math class, she might pose a question to the class.

"Students," she would ask, "how many apples would you have left if you had seven apples and then someone took away three apples?"

"I know, Miss Oppenheimer! I know!" I would yell, raising my hand as high as I could.

"Okay, Joe, how many would you have?"

"Eight," I would yell, just saying the first thing that popped into my head.

"No," she would say, with a slight frown, and then she would call on a smart kid who would know that the answer was four.

(It should be noted that my mom accompanied me to school the first day of class to make sure the teacher knew I preferred to be called "Joe," and not "Francisco" or "Francis.")

I didn't care if I looked stupid. I just wanted her to say my name and look at me. I had lost all concern for being seen as the dumbest kid in class. What did I care what the kids thought? For all I knew, we might move again after the year was over. I only cared about what Miss Oppenheimer thought, and even if I wasn't interested in learning anything in school, I did learn some of life's most important lessons that year.

Those lessons didn't come in class, but at the movie theaters. We had recently gone to the movies to see two Disney classics. The first was *Pinocchio* and the second was *Snow White*. I was totally taken with the beautiful lady who lived in the woods in a small cabin with seven men. That didn't strike me as being the least bit unusual.

What caught my attention in *Snow White* was that she was particularly fond of a dwarf named "Dopey." She would even kiss him on the forehead. Something I would have liked. He was the dumbest one, and he was my favorite, because I could relate to him. That love affair gave me the idea that if you want the girl, you should be just like Dopey. It came to me like a bolt out of the blue. It's what you might call a *gran idiota*, which means a "great idea." I became obsessed with being the dumbest kid in class—a task at which, as you shall see, I excelled at.

The other Disney creation, *Pinocchio*, left a lifelong impression in my psyche and shaped my idea about the difference between right and wrong. The movie, *Snow White*, confirmed for me a lesson I had learned in the first grade. That lesson was that girls and women like dumb boys, so I resolved to stay dumb as long as possible. The upside to that was that it would be a lot easier to be dumb than to get smart, I thought.

In *Pinocchio*, the lessons were much more complicated. As you may recall, Pinocchio was a wooden puppet who was carved by an old man who wanted more than anything to have a real boy because he needed help in his shop where he was way behind in his shoe business. One day a fairy princess came to the shop and waved her wand and brought Pinocchio to life, but he was still a puppet. To become a real boy, he had to first learn to be a good boy. (A subject that was heavy on my mind at that time.) Since he had been made of wood, he hadn't learned anything about being a boy. He was dumb, just like me and Dopey! This is one of the reasons that I loved that movie. Dopey, Pinocchio and I were three of a kind. We had a lot in common!

To see if he had what it took to be a real boy, he was sent off to school, just like me, and had to get smart so that he wouldn't make mistakes, like so many little boys do. But one day a bunch of hooligans approached him and tried to tempt him to go with them to do bad things, instead of going to school. (I had been there before.) At this point in the movie, I was getting a bit tense, thinking, "Don't go with them, Pinocchio! Don't go." But, as you may know, Pinocchio was not very bright, so he decided to go with them. "Where would they go?" I wondered. Maybe it was to the train tracks or to a fire escape. But no, it was much worse. They took him to an amusement park. Well, actually, I didn't think that was so bad. I've done worse.

But, as it turned out, this was not just any amusement park; this was a place where boys were told to do bad things, like smoke cigars and play pool, and drink beer. "No!" I screamed to myself. "Don't do it, Pinocchio!" I couldn't believe that my whole life was playing out before me on the big screen. Because of my experiences as a dumb kid who was led astray by hooligans, and who had been duped into not going straight home after school, I could see where this story was going.

Pinocchio didn't listen to me. Instead, he really got into it and started drinking, smoking and playing pool with the bad boys. He was having a great time, which is something I could relate to. Well, even I could see this was not going to end well. It was quickly turning into a horror story, one that I would never forget. The amusement park was full of good boys who had been lured there by the bad boys and as they played pool, smoked and drank, something horrible began to happen. They began to grow tails and long ears! Donkey tails and donkey ears! Could there be anything more horrible? Well, it turned out there could be.

The more they played and enjoyed themselves, the more they turned into donkeys. When the transformation was complete, they ceased to be boys any longer. They became donkeys! They couldn't even speak anymore; they would just bray like donkeys when they cried out for their moms to come and get them. YIKES!

And then, they would be herded together, loaded on trucks and taken on a long ride to the mines, where they would become slaves and forced to work for the rest of their lives. This is such a gruesome tale that I don't think little kids should be allowed to see it, but I guess Walt Disney knew what he was doing because the movie had, what I now believe to be, the desired effect on me. It scared the Holy Jesus, Mary and Joseph out of me. I knew at that moment that I was going to do my best to be a good boy from then on, if not the smartest one. That decision stayed with me the rest of my life.

Fortunately for Pinocchio, he was able to escape before he turned completely into a donkey, but he still had donkey ears and a donkey tail, and occasionally, when he tried to speak, he would just make a "braaaaaying" sound, like a donkey makes. What a horror. I would be so embarrassed! And then there was the problem with the nose. As you probably know, Pinocchio's nose would grow longer every time he told a lie. Because he wasn't very smart, he told a lot of lies and so his nose kept growing and growing until it looked like tree branch and a little bird made a nest on it. The nose thing really scared me because I had told some real whoppers in my time. What a mess Pinocchio was in.

However, it all ended well for Pinocchio. Thank God. He learned hard lessons; he lost his ears and tail; he got his nose back to normal; and he became a real, good (but maybe a little dumb) boy. He lived happily ever after, working feverishly the rest of his life making shoes from morning until late at night. I bet his father started making more boy puppets so he could expand his business!

But if all ended well for Pinocchio, I was still left with a constant worry that I might suffer the same fate. Each morning when I awoke I would run to the bathroom to check myself in the mirror to make sure I hadn't started growing donkey ears or a long nose. When bathing, I would check out my little *pompis* to make sure I hadn't started growing a tail. This obsessive behavior lasted throughout my elementary school years. After all, I had done a lot of naughty things in my younger days, and it was possible that "donkeyitis" was like some diseases that creep up on you and get you later in life.

No matter that I had vowed to be a good boy, I still hadn't gotten much smarter, which was ok with me because being dumb didn't require as much work as being smart. Also, I was still trying to woo Miss Oppenheimer by bringing her apples every day. I thought about writing a little love note to go along with the apple, but since I couldn't write yet, I would have to get someone else to write it for me and I couldn't think of anyone I could trust with that secret mission. Certainly not my sister!

Finally, as the school year was ending, I had another *gran idiota*. I would win her over by making her laugh. Yeah, that was it. I had to come up with a good joke. But where would I get one. The only ones I knew were the ones my grandfather told me, but they were all in Spanish, the forbidden language. I started asking other kids in class if they knew any good jokes, but their jokes were pretty lame. The best they could come up with was: "Why did the chicken cross the road?" Duh! Everyone knew that one.

So, one day at lunch I found what could be my salvation. At the candy counter, where I usually bought Jawbreakers or Red Hots, I saw a box of candy that had a riddle or a joke on the back. The answer to the riddle, it said on the box, would be on the tab. You had to buy the box and open it to see what the answer was. I think the candy was called Pom Poms. They advertised a chewy caramel center, covered with a layer of chocolate. Well, it was worth a try. I purchased a box after lunch, and on the back was the riddle: "How do you keep a fish from smelling?"

Before opening the box I tried to see if I could answer the riddle on my own. However, as I wasn't very smart, I gave up quickly and opened the box. As I popped a Pom Pom into my mouth and began to chew the yummy chocolate and caramel center, I checked the tab. The answer was: "Open at other end." I started to laugh because this was obviously supposed to be a very funny joke, but then I realized that I didn't really understand the answer. "How do you open a fish at the other end?" I wondered. "Which end of a fish are you supposed to open in the first place? How does that keep it from smelling?" Well, I pondered my new-found joke long and hard as I walked around the playground in a chocolate and caramel haze. Every once in a while I would stop a kid at random and pop the joke on him, just to see the response.

"Hey Jimmy," I would say, "Do you know how to keep a fish from smelling?" I would ask. Inevitably the answer was "No." Then I would give him the answer and he would kind of laugh, but then he would make a face as if he had just bit into a sour candy. He didn't get it. "Maybe," I thought, "El Paso kids don't know much about fish because they live in the desert and had never spent much time around fish." I knew I hadn't. I pondered the answer to the riddle for a couple of days and when the box was empty I tossed it into the trash. But the riddle remained my number one joke and I felt sure Miss Oppenheimer would get it because she was smart and would be able to figure it out right away.

One day, shortly after I found my joke, an opportunity presented itself in class. I am not sure what the subject matter was that was being discussed, but there was suddenly a lull in the conversation, so I raised my hand real high and yelled out, "Miss Oppenheimer, Miss Oppenheimer, I have a joke to tell."

This got her attention and she said, "Okay Joe, go ahead and tell your joke."

So, I stood proudly and said, "How do you keep a fish from smelling?"

There was a long pause as she mulled this over in her mind. Finally, she said, "I don't know, I give up."

This was great. She didn't know. I would be the first one to tell her this joke. So I said, "Open at other end," with great satisfaction.

The punch line did not have the effect I expected. Instead of laughing, she just stood there with a puzzled look on her face. No one in the class laughed either. There was just a deafening silence. "What had I done wrong?" I asked myself. It wasn't my fault that it wasn't funny. It was those darned Pom Poms. It was the fault of the company that makes up those stupid riddles. Eventually, she smiled and thanked me for my participation in class and then she continued where she had left off. I sat down, deeply humiliated.

If there had been any doubt about who the dumbest kid in class was, there wasn't any longer. So right then and there I realized where I had gone wrong. My decision to be the dumbest kid in class, like Dopey in *Snow White*, had not worked out well. I had to start getting smarter, and so, that very day after school, I turned over a new leaf. I did something very out of character—something I had never done before. I went straight home, sat down at the kitchen table, and actually did my homework.

(Author's note: If there is anyone who knows how to keep a fish from smelling, or which end of a fish is the correct one to open, please communicate the answer to the email address at the back of this book. It would be greatly appreciated.)

Joe and Helen Lewels in Juárez (1949).

ON the RIO GRANDE

4

Chapter *Cuatro*

Growing up Kind of Mexicany

By now you must have figured out that even though everyone calls me "Joe," my real name is Francisco Jose Lewels Cisneros. Cisneros is my mother's maiden name, which is used in Mexico to distinguish me from everyone else on the planet who is named Francisco Jose Lewels.

I sure wouldn't want to get mixed up with all those other guys. Some of them may be bank robbers, murderers, terrorists or maybe even dumb billionaires running for president. As it turns out, I really didn't have to worry about it because I was pretty sure the only other Francisco Jose Lewels was my father, but his mother's maiden name was Oviedo, so he was Francisco Jose Lewels Oviedo. The main reason there aren't any more of us around, anywhere, is that the name "Lewels" is very unusual, and after my experiences with the name, I was not about to name my kid "Francisco Jose"!

Although my dad's family also fled Mexico during the Revolution, the name Lewels is not Mexican, it is German. My great grandfather, Johannes Lewels (1824-1889), left Hamburg, Germany, around 1850 and emigrated first to the U.S. and then to Mexico. He ended up in Mazatlán, Sinaloa, Mexico, which is a beautiful beach resort that was then, and still is, an important port city on the Pacific coast of Mexico. There he met and married a young Spanish woman by the name of Rafaela Zepeda. He was 38 and she was 18. Together they had ten children who were born in Mazatlán, about one child every two years (poor woman), and then she died in childbirth with her 11th at age 40.

One of these children was my grandfather, Agustín, who I never met because he died in Mexico City in 1925 when my dad was ten years old. By then, my grandmother, Carmen, had five children to care for and no income. The family moved in with relatives in Nogales, Arizona, where my father had been born in 1915. This was the second time the family had to leave Mexico. The first time, around 1912, was when they fled the terror of the Revolution. The second was for economic survival. These were desperate years for them and the Great Depression was right around the corner. When it arrived, the kids were pulled out of school so they could help support the family. My dad was put on a train at age 15 and sent to El Paso to live with friends of the family.

It's not hard to understand why my dad never liked to talk about his childhood or his father. I am sure he and his family were all traumatized by the death of my grandfather, as well as by their desperate journey back to the U.S. to be with her relatives. And I can only imagine how my father must have felt when he was put on a train to go live in a strange city. Because he didn't like to talk about his childhood, I had to piece together his story from the few facts that were available. For example, while studying European history in high school, we learned the names of those who ruled the various nations in the past. One of the names was "Franz Joseph," Emperor of Austria, King of Hungary, Croatia and Bohemia 1830-1916. His younger brother, "Maximilian," reigned for a brief three years as the French emperor of Mexico, but was finally killed by a Mexican firing squad in 1867 when the French were ousted.

"Hmm," I wondered, "could there be a connection between my name and the Emperor of Austria?" After all if you translate "Franz Joseph" into

Spanish it becomes "Francisco Jose." And, I did have an uncle, my dad's brother, who was called "Max," short for "Maximiliáno." I went home that day and engaged my father in a conversation about our family history.

"Dad," we are studying about Emperor Franz Joseph of Austria in school and I was just wondering if our names, 'Francisco Jose', are in any way connected to him."

"Oh sure," he said. "I thought you knew."

"No," I said, "I don't know, because no one ever tells me anything about our family history."

"Well, our family is from Hamburg, Germany, you knew that didn't you?"

"Yes, I knew that," I said "but Franz Joseph wasn't German, he was Austrian." I countered.

"Well, I guess your grandfather, Agustín, just liked the Austrian royal family and so he decided to name his children after them."

"But Franz Joseph single-handedly started World War I by deciding to invade Serbia because someone killed his nephew, the Archduke Franz Ferdinand, who he didn't even like, thus causing the deaths of millions of people!" I cried.

There was a long silence as my dad contemplated the significance of what I had just brought up, and then he said, "Well, don't worry," he consoled me, "I don't think anyone will blame you. After all it was a long time ago. Look how long it took you to figure it out."

"Don't worry," was part of my dad's motto. "Don't worry and don't hurry," were the words he lived by. But not me. No, by then I was an "always hurry and always worry" kind of guy. So his attempts to calm me down often only made me angry.

"Well, you should have told me a long time ago that I was named after a mass murderer!"

"It just didn't seem important I guess," he said. "A name is just a name, after all."

"Well, that may be, but it could have had something to do with our family being chased out of Mexico by Pancho Villa, don't you think?"

"Oh, sure," he said. "The Revolution was all about the lower classes, which were mostly those with Indian blood (Mestizos), killing or getting rid of people of European descent, like us. It was also about overthrowing the government of the dictator, Porfirio Diaz, who ruled for 35 years."

"Your great grandfather, Johannes Lewels, left Germany around 1850 and ended up in Mazatlan, where he married and raised a family," he continued. "The name 'Lewels' marked us as Europeans, but that wasn't the only reason our family had to leave Mexico," he said.

"What else was there?" I asked.

"You see, your grandfather worked for the Porfirio Díaz regime. He managed a large plantation in the Yucatán Peninsula near the town of Mérida. It was a hemp plantation. It's called *sisál* in Spanish and it was used to make rope and sacks."

"Oh God!" I exclaimed. "That would have made him a big target for the revolutionaries."

"Yes," my father agreed, getting a little misty eyed. "He spoke five languages and was educated in Germany."

"So it wasn't just the name," I said, "but being named after Austrian and French royalty couldn't have helped."

"No," I guess not," he said.

Agustín Lewels Zepeda (center), wife Carmen and family in Mérida, Yucatán, Mexico (circa 1910) at their hacienda just before the Revolution.
Mariano Oviedo, my great uncle sits at left.

After much consideration, I relented a bit. Maybe he was right. A name is just a name, but I decided that if I ever had kids, I would name them simple, American names that would make their lives easier than mine had been.

It did get me thinking though about where I stood. Was I a German? Was I a Mexican, or was I an American? I thought maybe I might be a Mexican-German, except I didn't like being called a "beaner schnitzel." That slur really hurt. Maybe Mexican-American was what I was, but by the time I reached middle school, I was feeling mostly like an American. Most of my heroes were American: Roy Rogers, Gene Autry, John Wayne, and Superman. But more importantly, English had become my primary language and my Spanish was getting a bit rusty. At home, or at my grandparent's apartment, when I was spoken to in Spanish, I would often answer in English. The school system, the movies and by 1952, television, had turned me into a little "gringo" (American.) I had grown to believe (erroneously) that the Spanish language was inferior to English and that my future depended on my ability to speak English fluently (correctly). I was getting less Mexicany each day.

I suppose this would be a good time to try to explain what I mean by the term "Mexicany." First, it isn't a real word. It is just a word I use to try to describe people who have some connection to Mexico. I understand there are those who might find my use of this word politically incorrect or even insulting, but I only use it in an effort to come to terms with who I am.

Here are some of the ambiguities I found in my attempt to reconcile who or what I was when I was growing up. One example is that on my dad's birth certificate, dated March 7, 1915, in Nogales, Arizona, he was listed by the doctor as being of the "Mexican race." But "Mexican" isn't a race. It should have said "Caucasian." Mexicans are mostly Caucasians and therefore, cannot be distinguished as non-white. (A large percentage of Mexicans have some Indian blood. They are known as "Mestizos" in Mexico, but are still Caucasians. There are also small numbers who are of African or indigenous descent.) Instead, it could be said that Mexicans are not generally Anglo Saxons.

On the border, we say, "Oh, he is an Anglo or she is a Mexican."

However, this distinction breaks down quickly as there are many Anglos whose families have lived several generations in Mexico and never interbred with the indigenous people. They have Anglo names and they speak both Spanish and English fluently. If you asked them, they would say they are Mexicans, but you wouldn't be able to tell by just speaking with them or looking at them. Also, you can't distinguish Mexicans by the color of their skin because many, with European roots, as with my family, are light skinned.

Some of my cousins who live in Mexico have blue eyes and very white skin. Some of my wife's family members in Mexico are distinguished by their red hair and blue eyes. She is of German and Spanish descent, but her ancestors arrived in Mexico many years ago and they considered themselves fully Mexican. Nor can you always tell by the language they speak. In Mexico, they have a derogatory name for Mexicans who have lost their ability to speak Spanish properly; they are called "*pochos.*" I'm not sure where that name comes from, but we all know what it means. I would certainly fall into that category.

My Spanish is okay, but not Mexicany enough to fit right in when I travel to Mexico. There are many ways you can slip up when speaking Spanish in Mexico. One of the tricks they have to catch *pochos* is to pay attention when they attempt to identify an object or any noun by its gender. You see, in Spanish, everything has a gender. (This is a rule I would abolish immediately if I were made emperor of Mexico! Then I would get out of there pronto, before I was shot by a firing squad!)

The general rule is that when the noun ends in the letter "a" as in "boca," which means "mouth." It is female. So, you would say "*la boca,*" or "*la señora.*"

But, there are many exceptions to the rule and these you have to learn with experience and then memorize. Some don't make any sense at all. For example the word for "problem" is "*problema,*" which would lead one to believe that it is feminine. However, some female grammar teacher long ago decided that problems should be masculine, so it is correct to say "*el prob-*

lema," even though it is obvious that problems should always be feminine. There are so many of these "gotcha," exceptions to the rule that a *pocho* doesn't stand a chance when he engages in a conversation with a real Mexican. I liken these to landmines that lurk unseen across the language of Spanish that make you cringe when you find yourself using a noun with which you are not that familiar. You might be in the middle of a conversation when words such as "insulation" or "plywood," suddenly come up. Are they masculine or feminine? What the heck are those words in Spanish anyway? It's not as if they come up in conversation very often. So, there you are stuttering and stammering, trying to not look stupid.

On the border you can just tell the Mexicany worker who is repairing a wall to "put in some insulation and then cover it with plywood," by saying: "*Pongale insulation y cubrelo con plywood.*" He would understand perfectly well what you meant. (For the record, the word for "insulation" is masculine as in "*el aislamiento*" and the word for "plywood" is masculine as in "*el contrachapado.*" But you would have to use the feminine gender if you said, "*la madera contrachpada,*" because the word for "wood" (*madera*) is feminine. Even a word as simple as "water" (*agua* in Spanish) can mess you up because common sense tells you it should be "*la agua.*" But you would be wrong again. It is correct to say "*el agua.*" Gotcha again!

When you grow up on the border, you can easily stop speaking Spanish and start speaking "Mex-Tex" or, as some say, "Spanglish," as in the example above. These terms refer to people who mix the two languages together and who will substitute an English word for a Spanish word they don't know, in the middle of a sentence. This is done so fluidly that they don't even realize they have done it. If you live on the border it isn't a big problem because people will understand you. But if you do it in Mexico, you are considered to be a *pocho*. You will never make it in business or high society. Unfortunately, there are too many people on the border who cannot speak either Spanish or English properly, and therefore, they are doomed to exist in that netherland I call Mexicany. They can only find success by living on the border or in a community with a large Mexican-American population.

To succeed in elevating oneself into a higher class of society in either country, one must learn to speak, read and write at least one of the two languages proficiently. Prohibiting the use of Spanish in the public schools did the trick for me, but today that is seen as not politically correct. In my opinion the change in this policy only prolongs the kid's assimilation into American society. On the other hand, being truly bilingual has many advantages, and holding on to the many excellent aspects of the Mexican culture is a good thing. One thing I love about that culture is the *abrazo*, or hug. People regularly greet friends and relatives with a hug, which, I believe, promotes good health and longevity. The food is irresistible, and the laid-back culture is a great reprive from the workaholic culture one finds in purely Anglo society. (I consider myself to be a lazy workaholic. My German side keeps telling me to "work harder, work harder!" But my Mexican side keeps saying "*mañana, mañana*.")

Many Mexican immigrants or their children have chosen to become full-fledged Americans and have chosen English as their primary language. Many have lost their ability to speak any Spanish at all. If they have Spanish surnames then they are Mexicany in my view. I don't see this as a bad thing. My kids don't speak very much Spanish, they don't have Spanish surnames and they are very light skinned, so whether they like it or not, they are just a little-bit Mexicany. There are also those who prefer to be called *Chicanos*, because they are proud of their Indian heritage, and those who prefer to be called *Hispanic*, to denote their Spanish roots. People have to make choices about who they want to be, but it is only human nature that others may see them differently. It is a quandary.

When I was a kid, it was hard to find good role models in the media who were Mexicans. In the movies, often the actors who portrayed Mexican heroes were not really Mexicans. The American actor, Wallace Beery, portrayed Pancho Villa in the Academy Award nominated film *Viva Villa* in

1934; Marlon Brando played the revolutionary hero, Emiliano Zapata; Burt Lancaster was cast as a Mexican in one movie and an Apache Indian another; and Eli Wallach played the dirty, untrustworthy, *bandido* in several movies.

Why not use Mexican actors such as Gilbert Roland or Anthony Quinn in these roles? They could actually speak Spanish! (Gilbert Roland had to change his name from Luis Antonio Damaso de Alonzo to get any roles in Hollywood. Anthony Quinn was Antonio Rodolfo Quinn Oaxaca. Both were born in the state of Chihuahua) It seemed to me Mexicans were never portrayed in a positive manner; they were usually the bad guys or the poor cowardly villagers who needed American gunslingers to protect them from the bad Mexicans, as in *The Magnificent Seven*. Or they were portrayed as lazy and stupid.

In commercials, Mexicans were made to look comical and dirty. For example, the folks who sold Arid Deodorant created a TV commercial that started with a scene in a desert setting. A band of ferocious-looking Mexican bandits, bullet-belts strapped across their chests, riding on horseback, galloped toward the camera. They were ugly, dirty, unshaven, and their sombreros were old and disheveled. They emerged from a huge cloud of dust and were called to a halt by their thick-mustachioed, fat-bellied leader. The camera zoomed in on him as he reached into his saddlebag and pulled out a spray-can of Arid Deodorant. He lifted up one arm, smiled slyly, and sprayed his underarm. An Anglo-sounding voice then says: "If it works for him, it will work for you!" The message was obvious: Mexicans stink more than anyone! Unbelievable!

Another example was when the Elgin watch company launched a nationwide newspaper ad campaign featuring a Mexican hero, Emiliano Zapata. In bold letters, above a photo of Zapata, it announced, "Your new Elgin is better than the Elgins Zapata was willing to kill for in 1914. It's a good thing Zapata is gone, he would be stealing Elgins as fast as we could make them!" Incredible! These ads, along with others, such as Frito Lay's "Frito Bandido," the Mexican cartoon bandit that would steal your Frito corn chips at gunpoint, eventually bit the dust when Mexican-American civil rights groups protested the negative stereotypes in the 1960s and 1970s.

Another of my favorite early TV shows was *The Cisco Kid,* featuring a Mexicany-sounding actor named Duncan Raynaldo. He was a good role model, as he was the hero who solved crimes and caught the bad guy. He even wore a fancy sombrero to show that he was a Mexican. Years later I found out he was actually Romanian. His sidekick, the diminutive and clownish Pancho Gonzalez was actually a real Mexican, or should I say Mexican-American. He was played by Los Angeles-born actor, Leo Carrillo, whose real name was Leopoldo Antonio Carrillo. He and Duncan Raynaldo also made a movie about the Cisco Kid called *The Gay Amigo.*

Actually, there had been several earlier movies about the Cisco Kid in which another American-born, Hispanic actor, Cesar Julio Romero, played The Kid. That movie was titled, *The Gay Caballero.* Go figure. It seems that American audiences of the time liked to believe that Mexican heroes were all gay, but not in a sexual way, of course.

No discussion of "Mexicany" heroes would be complete without mentioning "El Zorro," (The Fox) the masked and dashing outlaw who harassed the tyrannical authorities in behalf of the poor in Los Angeles during the era of Mexican rule (1821-1846). The caped crusader's real identity was "Don Diego de la Vega," a Californio nobleman who was invented in 1919 by pulp-fiction writer Johnston McCulley. In the 1950s TV series, Zorro was portrayed by a definitely non-Mexicany actor by the name of Guy Williams. Over many years, many Anglo actors played this Mexican hero. Among them were Douglas Fairbanks, Tyrone Power, Alain Delane, Duncan Regeherd, and Anthony Hopkins. George Hamilton played Zorro in a motion picture titled (yep, you guessed it) *Zorro, the Gay Blade.* In this case the reference did have a sexual connotation.

I guess the point is that there were plenty of good actors of Mexican origin, who could actually speak Spanish, and who could have done a better job of portraying Zorro, Pancho Villa, Emiliano Zapata, or even a Mexican bandit, but apparently American movie studios didn't see any problem with Marlon Brando, Wallace Beery, Burt Lancaster, George Hamilton or Eli Wallach playing these roles on the big screen.

But for a little Mexicany kid who was trying to figure out where he stood in the grand scheme of things, it was terribly confusing.

Joe playing "The Cisco Kid." Circa 1951.

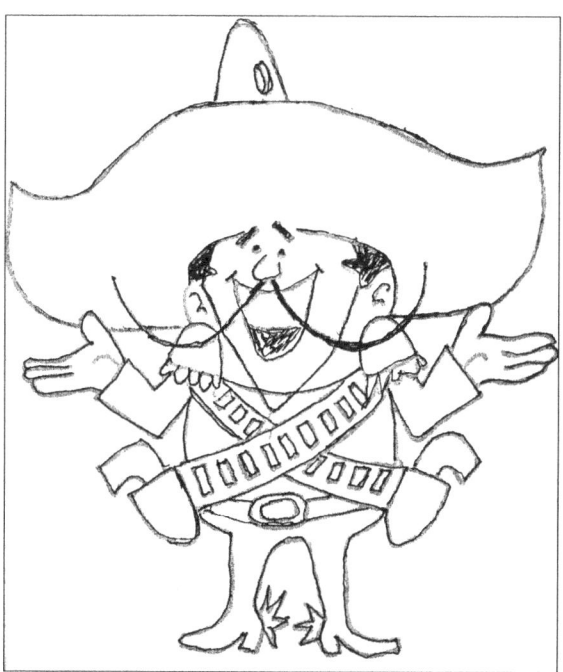

The Frito Bandido—he'll steal your corn chips!

ON the RIO GRANDE

5
Chapter *Cinco*

The Other Francisco

The name "Francisco" is a common one in Mexico. I know several men named Francisco and as we are friends, we say that we are "t*ocayos*." A *tocayo* (or *tocaya* if you are a female,) is a person with the same name as you, so when you meet someone who has the same name, you can say, "Oh you are my *tocayo*, or we are *tocayos*." There are also common nicknames for men named Francisco. They are often called "Paco," or "Pancho."

However, there is one "Francisco" I would never have called my *tocayo*. That person was Francisco (Pancho) Villa, the bandit and murderer who drove my family out of Mexico. To many people in Mexico he is a revolutionary hero who helped oust the dictator, Porfirio Diaz, but to my family, he was just a wonton killer. And if anyone should know the truth of it, it would be my dear *abuelitos*, Vicente Cisneros and Aurora Muñoz de Cisneros, for they were first-hand witnesses to the terror that Villa brought down on their small town of Jiménez, Chihuahua, Mexico, beginning in 1912 when the revolution had entered its third year.

My grandfather, Vicente, was born in 1888 in Jiménez, the year after his family moved from Guadalajara in the state of Jalisco. His future wife, my grandmother, Aurora Muñoz, was born in Jiménez a year later, in 1889. At the start of the revolution in 1910 she lived there with her father, Carlos Muñoz, (a widower who owned a general store) and her older sisters, Maria and Carolina. She also had two brothers, Eduardo and Jose ("Pepe"). The year 1910 was also the year that my grandparents were married, their reception held at an old adobe building called, flatteringly, "The Casino." Their first child, my uncle Vicente Carlos, was born there in 1911 and his sister, Refugio (mercifully nicknamed "Cuca,") was born in 1913, just before the family fled for the border. Their lives were full of joy and hope just as the dark clouds of war bore down upon them. Their lives were about to change forever.

Jiménez was just a small village of no great importance in those days; it was one of those towns that spring up on main thoroughfares that link major cities. In this case, Jiménez was located on the main road and railway between Mexico City and the border town of Ciudad Juárez. The railway ran from Juárez, south for 230 miles to the city of Chihuahua (the capital of the state of Chihuahua), on to Jiménez another 100 miles and then to the city of Torreón in the state of Coahuila, another 100 miles or so. From there it was nearly 900 miles farther south to the nation's capital, Mexico City, also referred to as "El Distrito Federal" (D.F.), meaning "Federal District. Unfortunately, the tiny town of Jiménez (which today in 2018 has a population of only 34,000) was looked upon by the revolutionary army, led by Pancho Villa, as a perfect place to quarter his army from time to time and plan attacks on the other major cities on the railway route. Another advantage for him was the fertile farm and ranch land that lay to the west of the town.

To understand how disastrous this was for the people of Jiménez and the rest of the state of Chihuahua, you first need to know what kind of man Pancho Villa was. Even though he rose to become General in Chief of the Northern Division of the Revolutionary Army, and is today heralded as a hero of the Revolution, Villa was in no way a man educated in the skills of warfare. In fact, by his own words, at the early age of 15, he killed the owner of a large hacienda where he and his family worked as sharecroppers. It is said that his motive had to do with his belief that the owner was about to rape his 12-year old sister. Then he fled into the mountains and gathered a gang of thieves who are said to have stolen from the rich landowners and helped the poor, much like the fabled Robin Hood. At least that is what many believe. One thing is for sure, according to his biography, *The Memoirs of Pancho Villa*, written by Martin Luis Guzman, Villa was "uncultured, devoid of schooling, and entirely illiterate. He rose from the abyss of banditry to the heights of great victory." His path to fame was a bloody one.

He was known for his great cruelty and his habit of personally executing anyone who he felt had disobeyed him or who was disloyal to the revolutionary cause. He was also known for his lust for women and for taking those girls who pleased him wherever he went. As he and his men paraded on horseback into a town, the women ran for shelter and the whole town shuddered in terror. It was truly unfortunate for my grandparents and their loved ones that Villa arrived in Jiménez in 1912 and began "requisitioning" provisions from the locals and conscripting men to join his army. The following year, in September 1913, the insurgent leaders of the state of Chihuahua met in Jiménez and elected Pancho Villa as their leader, making the residents understandably nervous.

The following month, Villa led his consolidated army of 10,000 men south to attack the city of Torreon, which was under the control of the counter-revolutionary General Victoriano Huerta. The battle was over quickly when Villa's troops unexpectedly overwhelmed Huerta's army and took Torreon. With the defeat of Huerta, Villa decreed the death penalty for any counter-revolutionary supporters, causing wild panic among the elite of the state of Chihuahua. A mass exodus of wealthy landowners, intellectuals and clerics headed for the U.S. border and the city of El Paso.

It was during this time that Villa's attention turned to the general store, owned by my great-grandfather, Carlos Muñoz, a blue-eyed, light-skinned man of Spanish descent. As the story was told to me by my grandparents, Villa's men walked into the store and demanded all provisions for the troops to be "requisitioned." Not only did Villa not like the looks of my great grandfather, but it is said he had heard that Carlos Muñoz had been speaking out against the revolution. So, when Carlos balked at Villa's orders, he was told he would have a few days to think about it. If he resisted he would be executed.

As my grandfather related to me, a few days after the warning, word came that Villa's men were coming to kill his father-in-law, Carlos. The day the assassins rode into town they caught Carlos off guard, walking across the main street in broad daylight. The soldiers rode up to him and fired numerous shots as they rode by. Then they galloped out of town.

Incredibly, they missed. Either they were drunk or they were just very bad shots, but the terrifying incident gave Carlos the final impetus to take action, and it gave the family a chance to escape. That night they piled everyone (four adults, two children and a newborn baby) into a horse-drawn wagon, took all the valuables they could carry and fled, not north to the border, but south to the city of Torreón, which, by then, was a safer route as Villa's army turned its attention north, to the cities of Chihuahua and Juárez. (By mid-November, Villa had taken the city of Juarez, cutting off safe passage to the north.) They knew that Villa's men would expect the family to flee north, toward the U.S. border, just as so many had done. They also knew that once Villa sentenced a man to death, there was to be no further negotiation or due process. If he was caught, he would be executed on the spot. (Fortunately, my grandmother's other brother, Pepe, had already fled to Mexico City and her two older sisters, Maria and Carolina had arrived safely in El Paso.)

The family was in a desperate condition. They had been forced to delay their departure until after my grandmother had given birth to her second child, Refugio/Cuca in November 1914. However, with the new baby only a few weeks old and with my grandmother still in no condition to be traveling on such an arduous journey they had to flee. If they had been able to go straight north, through the cities of Chihuahua and Juárez, the trip would have taken only a few days as the distance was about 330 miles. Under normal conditions, they would have taken the train. However, because that route had been denied them, they had to take a much longer and treacherous route of about 450 miles, which included crossing a large swath of the Chihuahuan desert. It was a perilous route, but they had no choice.

The journey nearly cost my grandmother and her newborn infant their lives due to extreme dehydration. The hardship caused my grandmother's breast milk to give out, putting her newborn's life in jeopardy. The whole group was nearly dying of dehydration as they finally reached the safety of the U.S. border by way of Laredo, Texas. They still had another 100 mile trek to San Antonio, where they remained for some weeks, recovering from the strain of their journey, and thankful to be alive. But, as it turned out, there would be one more final journey to be made. Work was hard to find in San Antonio, as it also had been deluged with refugees, so it was decided they would go west to El Paso, another 550 miles. My aunt Cuca was barley three months old when they finally arrived in El Paso in early March, 1915, thus making the total time spent on their long ordeal about 100 days.

Shortly upon arrival, Carlos wasted no time and opened a small grocery store at 625 South El Paso Street, a few blocks north of the international bridge. My grandfather, Vicente, found employment as a clerk in the linen department of the Popular Dry Goods Company, where he worked for nearly 45 years. There wasn't a housewife in town who didn't know him, as he was the one who sold them their sheets, pillow cases, and blankets for almost half a century. Later that year, on December, 30, 1915 their third child, my mother Aurora Elena, was born—a natural born U.S. citizen.

Back in Jiménez, things weren't going so well for those who couldn't leave. In Villa's memoirs, he tells the story of a young woman whom he coveted and whom he was determined to bed. He explains his compulsive behavior in this way:

"Chiefs of great armies are only men. They cannot always control their impulses or unworthy purposes…In Jiménez… I met a very nice family by the name of Del Hierro, an aunt and two nieces…Anita the older and Conchita, the younger….As Conchita was beautiful of body and eyes and coloring, I was attracted and soon fell in love with her."

The aunt met with Villa and said, "It is a pity that you are married, Sr. General."

"Why is it a pity?…It happens, senora, that marriage is one thing and love is another." he answered.

According to Villa's version of the story, and that is the only version that exists today, the aunt made a deal. She swore that Conchita was a great admirer of Villa and that she bore affection toward him. If Villa could assure her well-being and that of her family's, she would deliver Conchita to him.

Villa continues the story, "…As I was very anxious to consummate the union…I insisted she make her promises good that very day." However, the aunt made him wait until she could be sure that the details of the contractual agreement were completed.

Eventually the union was consummated, but Villa was not happy. He suspected the aunt had deceived him regarding Conchita's consent. Villa, in his memoirs, says "She (Conchita) talked of nothing but her dishonor, and when not telling me, she let me understand in other ways. She locked herself in the room we were occupying and wept all day….Many days and nights passed in this way; she weeping and bemoaning her shame and dishonor and I searching my conscience for proof of my crime."

Villa asked his confidant, Luisito, "Isn't it honor enough that Pancho Villa, being married already, chooses a woman and loves her and wins her and cherishes her?"

"Your wife is in Chihuahua my General," Luisito reminded him.

"…the honor of my marriage is there, and the honor of my love is here," he responded. "I just wanted Conchita to stop looking at me in horror."

In spite of these problems, Conchita traveled with him by train as far as Mexico City where he resolved to rid himself of her. "I began to wonder what the outcome could be, for Conchita had not only failed to respond to my affection, but looked on me with horror, as she was a woman of delicate spirit who easily gave way to tears when she was wounded…As it happened (a man) offered to sell me a matching set of jewelry." He purchased the jewelry and "I placed them in Conchita's hands without opening the case and said, 'Conchita, accept this and whenever you look at it, remember what a horrible fellow I am.' When several days had passed and she had not returned the gift, my conscience was at ease, and I had no scruples about sending her home, which I did."

The story ends there. We don't know what happened to poor Conchita after Villa took her honor and sent her back to her aunt in Jiménez. He continued to lead his revolutionary army in many battles throughout the northern states. But the tale, told in his own words, leaves no doubt that Villa was a self-deluded narcissist and sociopath who believed that everything he laid eyes on should be rightfully his, including the beautiful young women in the villages he passed through. He acted as policeman, jury, judge and executioner at a moment's notice, never looking back with remorse on the any of the executions he carried out.

Did my grandparents know poor Conchita and her family? I am not sure, but in such a small town I would guess that they did. I don't remember hearing them talk about her specifically, but they did talk about the many other young women Villa was said to have taken as his own throughout the years of the Revolution and his many wives.

To those who consider Villa to be a hero, all I can say is that I understand. The dictator, Porfirio Díaz, was a despot and the lower classes, primarily Indians and mestizos were kept impoverished and were constantly preyed upon by the ruling class who were mostly of European descent. Things needed to change. But the ends are not always justified by the means and a great many innocent people suffered greatly due to Villa's brutality. Many of those who survived were relieved when Villa was ambushed and assassinated in 1923, even though the revolution had ended three years earlier.

Seven gunmen riddled his car with 40 bullets as he was leaving his 25,000 acre hacienda near the town of Parral. One of the assassins was killed and the rest were caught the next day. However, only two of them served a few months in jail. There are several theories about who was behind the attack, but it most probably had to do with fear that Villa would reenter politics in the upcoming presidential elections the following year.

Mexican Revolutionary soldiers standing on the banks of the Rio Grande facing towards El Paso. Circa 1911. Three major battles were fought in Ciudad Juarez during the Mexican Revolution (Credit: El Paso County Historical Society.)

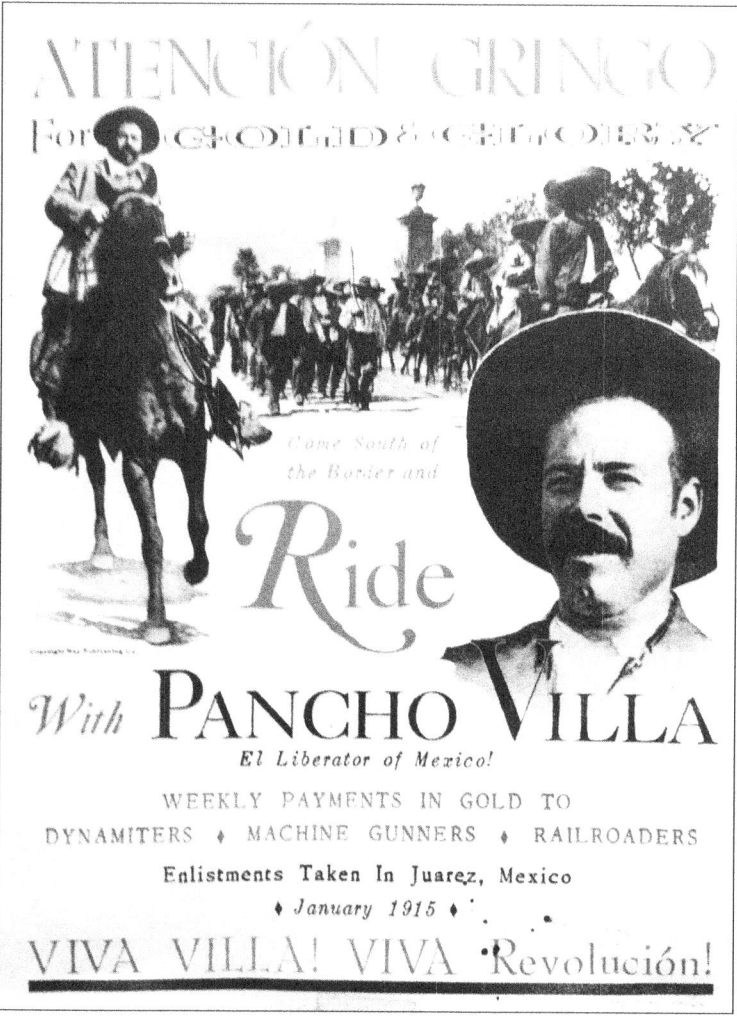

Recruitment posters (the social media of their day), like the one above, were plastered on walls in downtown El Paso in 1915. (Credit: El Paso County Historical Society.)

ON the RIO GRANDE

6
Chapter *Seis*
The Poor Mexican

Often my *abuelito*'s stories would begin with these words: "*Habia un pobre Mexicano.*" (There was a poor Mexican.) The family would know he was about to tell one of his many stories that revolved around his favorite subject: the poor, downtrodden Mexican who never caught a break. In spite of my grandfather's middle-class status in Mexico, he always sympathized and felt akin to the working class Mexicans who were mired in poverty.

When he got into his story-telling mood, we would all gather around him in the living room at the Faywood Apartments and settle in to be entertained. My *abuelita* would begin giggling when he uttered his famous introduction:

"There was once this very poor Mexican named Pedro who lived in a small village in the state of Chihuahua. His life was very hard because he worked in the fields all day and he couldn't even afford to buy a pair of shoes. Then one day he couldn't go on anymore and he died. He found himself standing in front of the Pearly Gates of heaven. They were the most beautiful things he had ever seen. They were so bright and shiny that he couldn't look at them without squinting, and they were so tall that he couldn't even see their tops.

"Standing in front of the closed gates were Saint Peter and the Archangel Michael who were there to greet the new arrivals. Pedro was embarrassed because his clothes looked like dirty old rags; he was covered with dirt from having plowed the field all day. His feet were filthy and he smelled of manure. Nevertheless, he took off his old, torn, sweaty sombrero and meekly walked up to Peter and simply said, 'Good Day Señor, I am here.'

"Pedro was smiling brightly as he looked up at St. Peter, and he waited to be greeted warmly, as he had been a good Catholic all his life. But Peter looked down at him with disgust and he scrunched up his nose so as not to have to smell the undesirable odors emanating from the poor Mexican. 'Sorry,' Peter said, 'but you can't enter here. You have to go to the other place. You know, down below.'

"Pedro tried to explain that he was a good Catholic and a good man who had never done anything bad, but had only worked hard in the fields all his life. However, his speech was interrupted by a great commotion. A large procession was arriving with a choir of angels and a band playing the Mexican anthem. Behind them came a golden carriage carrying a wealthy Mexican who Pedro recognized as the owner of a great hacienda who had contributed large sums to the Church when he was alive. St. Peter and the angel brightened up considerably as the great procession arrived, and they stepped forward, pushing Pedro aside, to greet the wealthy Mexican.

"After the greeting and a speech of gratitude by St. Peter, the huge Pearly Gates opened slowly and the procession of angels, the band and the carriage moved past the gates and into heaven. When the great gates closed once again, Peter and the angel Michael took their posts again, but something seemed amiss. Peter looked around and then he asked Michael, 'Where is that poor Mexican? Did you notice if he went down below?'

'No' answered Michael. 'I didn't notice.'

'Oh my,' said Peter. 'What if he slipped through the gates during the pro cession? How will we ever find him? God is really going to be angry when he finds out.'

'Don't worry,' said Michael. 'I have an idea how we can find him. We will wait until this week's *fútbol* (soccer) match. He will certainly be there.'

"You see, *abuelito* explained, in heaven they have soccer games every Saturday because even the angels and the saints get bored up there. They get tired of just sitting on clouds and playing their harps. You can imagine how boring that would be. So up in heaven there is a huge stadium big enough to hold all the angels, the saints and the good souls, and every nation is represented. Just before the game the band plays the anthems of every country and God gives a little pep talk. So, on Saturday when the stadium was full and the speeches were over, the band began to play the anthems. Of course they started with the American anthem and all the Americans stood and placed their hands over their hearts with great reverence and solemnity."

At this point my grandfather would stand and very seriously place his hand over his heart and hum "The Star Spangled Banner." This would get everyone laughing. Then as the German anthem was played, *abuelito* would stand with his arm held out like a Nazi salute and hum something that sounded quite German. He did this for the French anthem, which he seemed to know. And finally, the very last anthem played was the Mexican anthem, which he knew very well. He stood, saluted and marched in place as if the Mexican flag was actually waving right in front of him. He had us all laughing hard by then. He then went on with his story:

"At this point, St. Peter and Michael were observing the Mexican section of the stadium with extra-careful attention. Suddenly, they noticed a lone Mexican on the very top row who was jumping up and down and yelling,

"Ay yay yay ya ya yaiiiii! Viva Mexico!"

(This is known as the *grito* or shout of the revolutionary.)

'There he is!' exclaimed St. Peter, pointing to the top row where there was a great commotion. 'Go get him and throw him out of here!'

Oh my grandfather truly loved Mexico, and even though he was run out of Mexico by revolutionary soldiers, his heart bled for the downtrodden, poor Mexicans. This story about the "Poor Mexican," and others like it, says a lot about how my grandparent's loyalties were split between caring deeply for the poor and at the same time, being the victims of the Revolution. My grandfather was never a rich man. He was of Spanish descent, but he worked as a clerk in his father-in-law's store at the time of the uprising—hardly a position of power. Although he was not about to let himself be conscripted into Pancho Villa's army, he still sympathized with the *campesinos* (field workers) who were disenfranchised and abused under the Porfirio Díaz dictatorship.

Díaz, who overthrew the duly elected government in 1884, confiscated the lands from the indigenous people and sold them to wealthy Europeans and other outsiders. This resulted in only two percent of the nation's population owning most of the land of Mexico. In the state of Chihuahua, for example, one man, Luis Terrazas, owned a two-million-acre ranch, which was worked primarily by indigenous and *mestizo* laborers, who were kept in abject poverty. Díaz also sold franchises to foreign companies to develop Mexico's mining industry. The riches of gold, silver, copper and other precious metals, therefore, accrued not to the people of Mexico, but to the foreign interests. The owners, with names such as Guggenheim and Hearst, accumulated great wealth as a result of this arrangement.

By 1909 pressure was building among the lower classes to create change by any means necessary, due to the cruelty of the Díaz regime towards the indigenous people and the great disparities in wealth between the upper class, made up mostly of Europeans and Americans, and the great mass of people living in poverty. When violence finally erupted in November, 1910, the people of El Paso could sit on their balconies or stand on the banks of the Rio Grande to watch the battles taking place in the city of Juárez where three major battles took place during the ten-year-long revolution.

The story of "The Poor Mexican" also reveals my grandfather's (and many other Mexican's) feelings toward the Catholic Church, which was firmly in control of the souls of the people of Mexico before the Revolution, but which came close to being thrown out of the country along with the elite. My *abuelito* was not a fan of the Church because, in his view, it didn't do enough to help the poor, but rather stood with the ruling class, from which it drew financial support. Many leaders in the years after the fall of the Porfirio Díaz regime held great animosity toward the Church and by 1917 a new constitution was enacted which penalized Catholics severely. Church properties were confiscated, public manifestations of Catholicism, such as processions on religious feast days, were banned, monastic orders were dissolved, Catholic schools were closed and priests, nuns and brothers were forbidden to teach in the public schools. By 1926, the new president, Plutarco Elias Calles, an avowed atheist, tried to rid Mexico of all superstitious beliefs and all religious practices by passing what is known as the "Calles Law," which sought to further separate Church and State by excluding clerics from political and public life and forcing them to register with the state.

Such extreme measures turned into another civil war, (known as the Cristero War) as popular demonstrations in favor of the Church turned violent. As many as 200,000 civilians and soldiers died between 1926 and 1929 as the government tried to prevent the Church from regaining the power it had before the Revolution. Eventually, it succeeded in secularizing the country, but the influence of Catholicism gradually grew and by 1940 Catholics had regained their civil liberties and the Church experienced a revival. Nevertheless, the concept of separation of Church and State is one that remains popular in Mexico even to this day and the story of "The Poor Mexican" still resonates in Mexican culture. (See *The Cristero Rebellion Between Church and State* by Jean Meyer.)

ON the RIO GRANDE

7

Chapter *Siete*
Abuelito's Secret

Did I mention that my grandfather, my *abuelito* Vicente, had a girlfriend? Well, that's what my mother told me shortly after my grandmother, Aurora, died in March, 1964 at the age of 76.

I found myself having an all-too-familiar conversation with my sweet, but suspicious, little mom. "No, mom, grandfather doesn't have a girlfriend," I said condescendingly.

"Oh yes he does," she insisted. "He's had her for a long time! It killed your grandmother."

"Grandmother died of heart disease, which she had for many years," I said.

"No," she said angrily, "she died of a broken heart."

"Well, I don't want to hear any more about this theory of yours because I love my grandfather and he needs us now that he's all alone. Don't ruin that for me!" I exclaimed, ending the conversation.

I was a sophomore at TWC at the time of my *abuelita's* death and my newly-widowed grandfather was living alone at the Pearl Apartments, just behind the old Sunset Grocery in Sunset Heights. He was sad, alone and miserable. Not only had he lost his wife of 54 years, but he had been forcibly retired from the Popular Department Store where he had worked since 1915, the year the family arrived in El Paso. He didn't want to retire. He was still strong and in good health, but he was told he had to retire for insurance purposes. They gave him a gold watch and a $92 per month pension. He never talked about it, but he must have born some bitterness toward the company he so faithfully served for so many years. He had to smile and cow tow to each new Anglo department manager that was hired, even though he was much more qualified for the job. The reason he was never promoted was that he was a Mexican, and that must have burned deeply.

For nearly 45 years he walked from Sunset Heights to the Popular in downtown El Paso every morning. Then he would walk back for lunch, which my *abuelita* had prepared for him with great punctuality. He would lie down for 30 minutes and then walk back downtown. At the end of the day, he would walk back home (a total walking distance of about 50 city blocks.) No matter the weather, he always wore a three-piece suit and a hat. He always looked like a gentleman. His greatest piece of advice to me as a child was: "*Los hombres deben ser feos, fuertes y formales.*" (Men should be ugly, strong and formal.) I tried to follow his advice, but I just couldn't live up to the "ugly" part. It wasn't my fault. I often wondered why men had to be ugly, but he never explained that part to me. For him, it was simply self-evident.

Anyway, all that walking and all that lifting of boxes at work had left him in very good shape by the time my grandmother died. He suddenly found himself with nowhere to go, nothing to do and no one to do it with. Out of habit, he would get up early each morning, put on his suit and hat and walk downtown. He would just walk around. One afternoon I happened to see him as I was driving through town on my way to work. My first impulse was to stop and say hello, but I was curious about where he was going, so I followed him for several blocks, staying out of sight. "Where the heck is he

Wedding Reception, Jiménez, Chihuahua, MX. 1910 at the Casino. At the top stands Vicente Cisneros Velasco. Seated before him in the white blouse is Aurora Muñoz de Cisneros.

going," I wondered. Then, he crossed a street, approached a Catholic Church, and went in. I was puzzled. My grandfather had obviously not been a religious man. I don't remember him ever going to mass or praying, so I didn't know what to make of it. Certainly he had been raised as a Catholic and my grandmother was a devout Catholic, she even had a large photograph of Jesus hanging over her bed. I once asked her if it was autographed. She got a good laugh out of that.

But to find out my lonely grandfather had been going to Church each day made me very sad for some reason. Had he turned to God in his grief? Was it just a cool place to pass the hot, summer afternoons? I didn't know and I couldn't ask because I didn't want him to think I had been tailing him, which I had.

I think of all the people around him I was the one who loved him the most unconditionally. Maybe it was that I didn't really know anything about him as a man, only as a grandfather. Anyway, I knew he loved me. He would take me to baseball games at Dudley Field in the summer. He loved baseball, but because I was barely four or five years old, I had little concept of what it was all about. We would take the bus to the ballpark and by the end of the game I would fall asleep in his arms and he would carry me back to the bus and then up the stairs back at our apartment.

On Friday nights, when I was a kid, we would all gather around the radio and, in later years, the television set in my grandparents' apartment and listen to or watch the "Friday Night Fights." Boxing was the favorite show in their place, and my grandmother was just as much a fan as my *abuelito*. She knew all the boxer's names and would be glued to the set to watch every punch and jab. (I told you those Chihuahua women are tough.)

I looked up to my grandfather and to me he was a hero. He worked hard, never missing a day, and he treated me like his special little king. I loved his stories and his jokes and I sat in awe as he ate his two eggs, sunny-side up, with two pieces of bacon and a piece of toast every morning. He would douse the eggs with hot sauce (a habit I acquired later in life) and chase it all down with a large cup of black coffee and one of his ever-present Lucky Strike cigarettes. Then he would put on his tie, his vest, his coat and his hat and leave for work. What better hero could a little boy have? I didn't want to hear anything bad about my grandfather, even if it was true. So, after my *abuelita* died, I would try to drop by and visit him when I had time during the school week or on weekends. It would always make his day. But one time I arrived late. It was getting dark but there were no lights on in his apartment. I decided to peak in the living room window to see if he was there. I was puzzled and then shocked to see him sitting in a chair, staring at a wall. The TV set was not on. He wasn't asleep. He was just staring at an empty wall. It was heartbreaking.

A year went by and I tried to cheer him up whenever I could, but he was clearly disconsolate. At this rate, I felt, he was not going to last long.

One Saturday my mom said she wanted to go over to see him as she had not been able to reach him by phone. I thought this strange so I insisted on going with her. When we arrived, we went to his apartment door and knocked. No answer. We went around to the living room window and peaked in, expecting the worst. But instead of a body, we couldn't believe the apartment was totally empty. He had moved out. We immediately went to the manager's office and inquired. The lady said he had moved out the day before and left no forwarding address. I couldn't believe it. It was a profound mystery that frightened me to the core. "Where could he have gone?" I asked my mom.

"Well, I think I know," she said mysteriously.

"So tell me," I asked impatiently.

"I think he's in Houston. I think he went to live with his girlfriend."

"He's 76 years old; how could he possibly have a girlfriend?" I challenged. In my mind people that old were way beyond the stage where they had girlfriends and boyfriends. It was beyond my reckoning to think such a thing.

"Okay, so why do you think he has a girlfriend in Houston?" I asked.

"She's not just a girlfriend," she said in all seriousness, "she's been his mistress for many years and I think they have a child who lives with her in Houston."

"What are you talking about?" I said unbelievingly. "This is the first I ever heard of it. If that's true, then why haven't I ever heard about it?"

"It's been a family secret. We didn't want the whole world to know."

"Who is 'we'?" I asked.

"Your aunt Cuca and uncle Vicente and I have known for many years. We even told him we knew, but he didn't care. He has been going to visit her for years and they have even taken vacations together," she asserted.

"I can't believe it. Where would he even find a girlfriend in Houston?" I asked.

"He didn't find her in Houston. She used to work with him at the Popular years ago. Everyone there knew about them."

"And grandmother?" I asked.

"She's always known. She has suffered all these years knowing her husband loved another woman. It broke her heart."

"Oh God," I said. This was just too much for me to digest all at once. "How could I not have known?" I asked myself. If this was all true, and I was beginning to believe it was, then I had been totally oblivious of the great secret all these years. My grandmother really was a saint. But what did that make my grandfather? It made him a stranger—someone I thought I knew but did not. I was overwhelmed with mixed emotions. On the one hand, I felt great sorrow for my poor grandmother who I had loved so dearly. But on the other, I somehow felt happy for my grandfather who was now in Houston, sharing his life with someone who cares for him. He wasn't alone, staring at the wall in the dark. "Oh man," I thought, "family secrets can really hurt people." I wondered if all families have secrets like ours. I decided that they do. All families have secrets—secrets that cause pain to all concerned.

It was about a month later that my mom got a letter in the mail. It was postmarked from Houston. It was from my grandfather. In it he explained that he had gone to live with the other woman and that he was happy. He apologized for all the pain he had put his family through and begged her forgiveness.

But my mom was short on forgiveness that day. She and her siblings would never find a way to forgive him, not even after he died.

In the letter, he said they were planning to travel by train through El Paso and on to California that summer and he would like to bring her to our house for a visit. That idea didn't hit a good note with my mom. She wrote him back saying he would be welcome to come by the house but that the woman would never be welcome. He said if he couldn't bring her, he would not come. They were at a total impasse.

The next month my mom told me that they had arrived in El Paso and were spending a few days at a hotel near the Union Depot. He invited us to go visit them. Of course my mom wouldn't have it, but I was eager to see my grandfather once more. There was no telling when I would have another chance to see him. So, after class the next day I went to visit him and the "girlfriend." By then they had married and, therefore, she was technically my step-grandmother. I had no idea what to expect. She was supposedly much younger than he and word was that she had been quite attractive years before. I just didn't care. I wanted to see him happy just one last time.

My *abuelito* opened the door with a big smile and a mighty *abrazo* (hug). "*Mi amigo don Pompeyo*," he said with tears in his eyes. I broke down sobbing with my head on his shoulder. It was as if he had died and come back from the dead. He would always be my dear *abuelito*, no matter what.

As I was clearing away the tears, I turned and saw a little old lady standing behind me. She stood about five feet tall and was considerably overweight, but she had a big smile on her face and she embraced me as if I were her long-lost grandson. I could tell she had heard a lot about me for many years. She too started crying and that got me going again. My grandfather put his arms around us and we all had a good cry. Without saying as much, I knew they were asking my forgiveness and without saying so, I forgave them unconditionally. She turned out not to be the beautiful girlfriend I had imagined.

She was just a little, old, fat, "Mexicany" woman who obviously loved my grandfather and that was all that mattered to me. I sat and visited with them for maybe half an hour and then I said goodbye and rushed off to work, knowing I might never see him again. I didn't care what he had done, I just wanted him to be happy for the rest of his life.

Years went by. I graduated college and the army kept me hopping from one base to another and then to Vietnam. I was in graduate school at the University of Missouri when I got a call from my mom. "Your grandfather and that woman were in a bad car wreck in Houston. He's in a coma and they don't know if he will live."

"In a car wreck?" I asked unbelievingly. "*Abuelito* never learned to drive and he never owned a car!" I protested. "How could that happen?"

"The woman was driving. Her sister called to tell me," my mom said.

"What about his wife?" I asked.

"She's okay. She was driving the car but she walked away unharmed," she said angrily.

"Are you going down there to be with him?" I asked.

"No. I'm going to wait to see what happens," she said.

"Okay, thanks for telling me. Please keep me posted. I'm in the middle of final exams and I can't leave."

A week went by and I got a call from my mom. "She's dead," she said.

"What do you mean? You had said she walked away unharmed from the crash."

"Apparently she had internal injuries. She seemed fine after the crash, but she really wasn't."

"What about grandfather?" I asked.

"He's still in a coma. The doctors will call me if he wakes up."

"Okay, call me with any news," I said.

A few days later he came out of the coma only to find out his wife was dead. I can't even begin to imagine the sorrow and the pain he felt. When he was well enough he was taken to live with the lady's sister there in Houston.

I had the opportunity to speak to him by phone shortly after, but he seemed very depressed, as you might imagine. I didn't think he would last long. Weeks later, he died in the arms of the woman who had been caring for him—a total stranger to us. None of his real family was with him at the time.

"How strange," I thought. "He died so far away from that little town of Jiménez where he met and married my grandmother. His own children had disowned him. I guess you can never know where your choices are going to take you, or who will be there with you when you die."

(For the record, there was no love child. That part of the story was just spun out of my mom's vivid imagination, the product of her ever-suspicious nature. It just simply wasn't true, but if it was, it would have made for a much better story.)

The Cisneros family in El Paso in 1917. Left to right: Aurora Muñoz de Cisneros (*abuelita*), Refugio (Cuca) Cisneros Muñoz, Vicente Cisneros Muñoz, Vicente Cisneros Velasco (*abuelito*), Aurora Cisneros Muñoz. (My mom.)

ON the RIO GRANDE

8

Chapter *Ocho*

"El Paso Girls are Stupid"

While going through my dad's papers after his death at age 81 in 1996, I was astonished to discover that he had become famous as a young boy and had even gotten his picture of the front page of the newspaper for saving people's lives.

It happened because he had taken night classes in business, typing and English and gotten a job as a copy boy at the *El Paso Post* (later *Herald Post*) shortly after arriving in El Paso in 1930. It was a menial job, but as fate would have it, he became the subject of a front-page story on one of his first days on the job. There had been a big fire at a downtown hotel and the reporter assigned to the story was calling all over town trying to find out who the mysterious person was who called in the alarm and then helped women and children, who were trapped in the upper floors, out through a window, onto a roof and into another hotel.

The front-page story in the *Post* the following day, accompanied by a mug shot of my dad, stated that the reporter yelled across the newsroom to the editor: "I can't find out who in the heck turned in the alarm!" My father, 16 years old at the time, finally spoke up and said, "I did that." The story headline read:

"Modest Joe, *El Paso Post's* One and Only Copy Boy, Scores Scoop."

The story starts out by saying, "If Joe Lewels, 16, office boy for The *El Paso Post*, ever gets over his modesty he may make a good reporter." It turned out that "modest Joe" had been on his way to work when he saw smoke coming out of the windows of a hotel. After turning in the alarm, he went in and started helping people get out. Once the firemen had the blaze under control, he went to work, but said nothing about the ordeal to anyone. After the story came out, every time the editor needed the copy boy, he would yell out "Hero" instead of "Boy" or "Copy."

"Modest Joe" went on to become not only a reporter, but the first reporter who could cover events happening in El Paso's sister city, Juárez, and throughout Mexico. He became the first Mexican-American and bilingual reporter for a daily newspaper in America, even though his readers were not aware of this. All his stories carried the byline, "by Joe Lewels," which sounded very much like an Anglo name. I believe this is what gave him the break he needed to succeed in what was then a very Anglo/white controlled media. He had adopted the nickname "Joe" to blend into American society while he was in elementary school, just as I had. He never told me if his mother had to tell his teachers to call him "Joe" or if he had an embarrassing episode, as I had, in the first grade. In any case, I learned that my dad and I had a lot in common. Even my choice to become a journalist was due to my dad's success as a reporter. When I was quite small he would take me to the newspaper offices downtown and introduce me to the editors and reporters. What impressed me the most was the room with all the teletype machines clattering away, spewing reams of (real) news stories about events happening all over the world.

El Paso Post—1931

The newspaper, in later years, sent him to Mexico City to cover the Mexican presidential elections in the mid-1930s and 1940s, and his work was picked up by the wire services, reaching national and international audiences. Later, he was offered the job as bureau chief of the Mexico City office of the United Press International wire service, but he turned it down because, by then, he was married and my mother wouldn't leave El Paso.

Eventually, he left the newspaper, but continued writing about Mexican politics as a "stringer" for the wire services. He found reporting satisfying, but the job just didn't pay enough to raise a growing family, so he tried his hand at various jobs and businesses with varying success. He met my mom (Aurora Cisneros), married her and raised three kids (Helen, Joe and David), all born in El Paso.

My mom, on the other hand, never felt the need to further her education and seemed content to be a housewife and a mother. When I think of her there are a number of adjectives that come to mind: loving, meek, fragile, supportive, beautiful, kind, shy, and feisty.

It still isn't clear to me why she dropped out of school after the fifth grade, but I think in those days it really didn't matter much. She told me she had health problems, but I think girls just weren't expected to be educated in those days and she didn't particularly like school. When I would ask her about it she would say there were girls who picked on her and that she had to fight them regularly. Even though she was always the smallest girl in class, she insisted that she was a good fighter. She showed me the proper way to "put up your dukes" by standing and posing as a professional fighter. I found this hilarious; even as an adult, her hands were the size of a five-year-old child. But, she claimed "I wasn't afraid of them. I could fight as hard as they could. But they would gang up on me."

As for me, I thought my mom was the most beautiful mom in the whole world. As a matter of fact, she looked kind of like Snow White herself, with porcelain-white skin and dark hair. She couldn't sing or whistle like Snow White though, as far as I knew. But she worked hard to keep the household together and she could make one heck of a "sheese" sandwich!

Once she told me a story about herself that, I think, says a lot about how this poorly-educated and very-sheltered young girl dealt with the world around her. When she was a teen, her mother took her on a trip to visit friends and relatives in Chihuahua City, about 200 miles south of El Paso. They were staying at the home of some friends who also had a teenage daughter named "Marta." The first thing my mom noticed was that Chihuahua girls were much more grown up than El Paso girls of the same age. They dressed better, acted more like adults, had smart sayings and believed themselves to be far superior to the girls on the border. They saw all border girls as "*pochas.*"

On the first night of their visit they all sat around the dinner table and as they were beginning to eat their meal, Marta declared loudly, "El Paso girls are stupid!" My mother told me that everyone stopped eating and the room got very quiet. No one said a thing. Everyone was looking at her.

"What was going through your head?" I asked.

"Well, I was thinking she was right," she answered.

"You thought she was right?" I asked in disbelief.

"Yes, I thought she was right. So I didn't say anything. I didn't even look up, I just kept eating my food."

"Well, didn't your mother stick up for you?" I asked.

"No, nobody said anything. They just started eating their food and pretended nothing happened."

"Why did you think she was right when she said that El Paso girls were stupid?"

"Well, I always thought Chihuahua girls were smarter because of the way they dressed and acted, so I really couldn't argue with her."

"That must have made the rest of the trip awkward for you. It must have been hard for you to be insulted like that on the first night you were there," I commented. "How did you deal with that?"

"Well, I just ignored it for the whole two weeks. I pretended like it never happened and just kept quiet. I tried to be friendly."

This story was just too funny, I thought to myself. It was just like my mom. She was very shy and quiet around strangers. You had to get to know her to see that she could be quite chatty and funny.

"So did you have a good time while you were there?" I questioned.

"Oh yes, we had a wonderful time. We went to parties and I met some really cute boys. They all wanted to dance with me. It was fun," she said.

"That's great," I said. "I think you handled it the right way. Getting into a fight would have ruined your vacation. So when you finally left, was Marta still being mean to you?" I asked.

"Oh no. We became friends. She was nice to me the rest of the time I was there. I got to meet her friends and we all got along. But when we were leaving and we were all in the car about to pull out, Marta came to the window and said, 'Why don't you invite me to come to El Paso sometime? It would be a lot of fun and I would like to meet some of your friends.'"

"Well what did you say to that?" I asked.

"Oh, I just told her she wouldn't like it there. She asked me why and I just said, 'You know, El Paso girls are stupid. You just wouldn't have any fun.' Then the car took off and I never saw her again".

"Well you really got her back. That is so funny." I said

"No," she responded, "I wasn't trying to get back at her. I liked her. I was just telling the truth. She wouldn't have fun in El Paso roller skating or playing kickball with my girlfriends and the kids in Sunset Heights. We were still kids and she was growing up too fast. I would have been embarrassed for her to see how I lived."

Now I understood. My mom didn't have a mean bone in her body. She just simply told the truth. Poor Marta was missing her childhood by trying to grow up too fast, while my mom was still just a kid. This story reminds me about how much I miss her now that she is gone. I loved the afternoons that we would sit and talk after my dad died and she was left alone for the first time in her life. She did so much for me; I could not have wished for a better mother. If I ever had a problem I couldn't solve, my mom would figure out a way around it. For example, when I graduated from high school and went to enroll in college, I found out I would need $150 for the first semester tuition. It doesn't sound like much now, but then it was a lot. My dad, whose business ventures were not going well at the time, couldn't help, so my mom took me to a pawn shop where she hocked her wedding ring to get me the money. I couldn't bear the thought that she would lose her ring, so after I enrolled, I got a job at a movie theater downtown and paid her back. From that day on, I never borrowed another dime from her or my dad. To be fair, my dad did buy me a used 1953 Chevy for $150 in my junior year of high school, and for that I am eternally grateful.

Life at home always had its ups and downs financially and it was also defined by my parents' many squabbles about money and jealousy. For example, there was the time my mom believed my father had a girlfriend named Alicia. Yes, that's right my dad had a girlfriend, at least my mom was sure of it. This happened while I was a freshman at Texas Western College (Go Miners!) and I was still living at home. My folks were in their early 50s and, I thought, a little too old to be having girlfriends or boyfriends, but their relationship had never seemed very mature to me. Possibly because they started dating in their late teens, they formed a relationship full of jealousy and mistrust. They each believed that the other was so attractive that members of the opposite sex were always throwing themselves at them. Maybe this was true; I just don't know. To put it as kindly as possible, I would say they had a stormy relationship throughout their marriage, and I would often get caught in the middle, with my mother unloading her troubles on me and causing me to become the reluctant referee.

"Your father has a girlfriend," my mom complained to me one day. "I am so mad at him. I want him out of the house. I want a divorce!" she declared.

"Mom, I am sure dad doesn't have a girlfriend. You're imagining this. Calm down"

"No, I am sure he does have a girlfriend, I even know her name. It's 'Alicia'. I want you to help me find a lawyer so I can divorce him!" Just as I was explaining to her how ridiculous she was being, my dad arrived and she laid into him.

"I want you out of the house!" she screamed.

"Where would I go? I don't have anywhere to go. Believe me I would if I could, just to get away from you!" he screamed back.

"Hold on, hold on," I butted in. "You've been married for almost 25 years and now you want a divorce? It's too late! You just have to learn to get along for a few more years. You should have gotten a divorce years ago. It would have made life easier for all of us. We are all tired of your constant bickering and we don't like getting caught in the middle of it." I scolded them.

"Well, if we don't get a divorce, I want to build a wall through the middle of the house so he can stay on his side and I don't have to see him or talk to him!" my mom said.

"Oh, that's a great idea," I said sarcastically. "Who would get the kitchen?"

"I would," my mom said, not missing a beat.

"You don't even cook!" my dad jumped in.

"This is crazy." I said. "Let's sit down and talk about this calmly." I ordered.

I finally got them to sit down and calm down. Then I began to play detective, just as in the movies.

"Dad," do you have a girlfriend?" I queried.

"No, of course not." He answered convincingly.

"Yes you do and her name is 'Alicia'!" my mother interjected angrily.

"Okay," I said. "Let me handle this. Dad do you know a woman named 'Alicia'?"

"No, I don't know anyone named 'Alicia'. Your mother is crazy. I don't know where she gets these ideas. This is how she has been all our lives. She's nuts!" my dad responded.

"I am not crazy," my mom interrupted again, "and I can prove it."

"Okay, Mom. How can you prove it? Show us the proof." I said, losing my patience.

With that, my mom got up and went into her bedroom and came out with an envelope and handed it to me. "See," she said. "It's addressed to "Jose Lewels" and it is signed by "Alicia." It arrived last week."

I examined the envelope and I could see she was correct. The envelope was addressed to "Jose Lewels" and it was sent to our address. The handwriting was clearly that of a woman's.

Inside was an Easter card and beneath the engraved greeting were the words: *"Para Jose, con amor."* (To Joe with love.) It was signed "Alicia." "You see," my mom said. It's true. I'm not crazy!"

My dad asked to see the card. "I don't know who this is!" he exclaimed. "I don't know anyone named 'Alicia.'" He was truly puzzled, but my mom was sure she had the smoking gun that proved her husband's infidelity.

"Wait," I said. "Let me see that card again." I examined the card carefully.

As I looked at it, a dim bulb lit up in the back of my brain, and then it grew brighter and brighter. Then I was certain I knew who the mysterious "Alicia" was. I had solved the mystery, but my mom was not going to like the solution.

"I know who 'Alicia' is," I said, pausing for effect. Now I had their undivided attention and I was savoring the moment. "This card is not addressed to dad, it's addressed to me." Now I really had their attention. "'Alicia' is a friend of mine. She's in my Spanish class at school. The teacher makes us speak Spanish and write in Spanish the whole time we're in class, so she calls me 'Jose' and I call her 'Alicia'. Her real name is Alice Steinman. She and I are always carrying on conversations in Spanish. She has a good sense of humor. She sent it to me as a joke, and not to dad. When she sent it she didn't know that my father's name was also 'Jose'. This is all just a silly mix up. Dad does not have a girlfriend. Case closed!" I said emphatically.

Needless to say, both of my parents were stunned, my mother most of all. She was absolutely speechless. My dad on the other hand laid into her. "You see, you are crazy. You completely imagined this whole story and you have been going around like a crazy woman for a week carrying that stupid card around. You should have just showed it to me and we could have figured it out right away!" he argued.

Of course, he was right. Too many years of suspicion and mistrust prevented her from doing the right thing when she first saw the card. She had jumped to conclusions and in the process caused the matter to get totally out of control. You can imagine how silly and stupid she felt to find out she was wrong and had been acting like a crazy person. Finally, she broke down in tears. She sobbed uncontrollably as she apologized. She said she wouldn't hire a lawyer and seek a divorce. "But, I still want a wall through the middle of the house," she declared.

"Oh dear God," I thought. "This is never going to end."

Actually, it never did. They stayed married for another 34 years, making a total of almost 58 years at the time of my father's death. She had become so dependent on him that she nearly had a nervous breakdown when he died. She sobbed and sobbed and sobbed. Finally, I reminded her that she really didn't even like him. But she just kept saying, "I want him back! What am I going to do without him? I can't live without him!"

But she did. She managed to live for another 15 years after his death, learning for the first time what it was like to be independent. It wasn't easy. She died at the ripe old age of 95. My poor little mom. God bless you.

And Dad, I am so glad you had a calm 15 years up in heaven. They must have been, well, heavenly. I hope by now the angels have interceded and accomplished what I could not. I pray that you two are finally getting along.

On the bright side, I did learn a very important lesson from my parents. I vowed never to allow jealousy into my relationships with women. A lack of trust will destroy even the most dedicated marriages. Once a spouse loses respect for his/her mate, it is nearly impossible to regain.

(Author's note: Although bickering was a way of life for my parents, there were also good times when they were behaving themselves. Sometimes they could even be "lovey-dovey." Their arguing never became violent, but the topic of divorce hung in the air like a dark cloud. The wall through the middle of the house was never built.)

Francisco Jose (Joe) Lewels Oviedo
(1915-1996)

Aurora Cisneros de Lewels (1915-2011)

ON the RIO GRANDE

9

Chapter *Nueve*
Getting Cool
(or) That fart changed my life

It was a beautiful summer evening in 1961 and I was sitting in my Chevy at the Bordertown Drive Inn Theater in far-east El Paso. At my side was a beautiful, blue-eyed blonde who had just recently moved to El Paso from Odessa, Texas—three hundred miles to the east. Holly was a sophomore and she was absolutely exuberant about being on a date with one of the popular boys (yes, you heard right). She had that little Texas drawl that was so cute, unlike the Midwestern accent that I, and most El Pasoans, had. Her eyes were always bright and her smile was radiant. I couldn't have been more delighted.

We had just gotten settled in, and after some light chit chat, we were starting to get down to a little necking, which was the whole purpose of going to the drive in. Then she said: "You know Joe, my daddy won't let me date Mexicans."

I know what you're thinking: "What the heck could he possibly say to that?" That's exactly what I was thinking. I was at a complete loss for words.

Was she just merely stating a random fact, or was she hinting she knew I was Mexican? I couldn't tell. She seemed much too naïve to be playing mind games, yet she had chosen a poignant moment to make that pronouncement.

I was buffaloed and totally speechless.

Her question was doubly puzzling because only a few days earlier I had been thoroughly vetted by her father. Holly asked me to come over to meet him and her mother to get their approval for the date. I arrived at the appointed time and she and her father were standing out in front of their house chatting. I got out of my car and walked over to them without any hint of nervousness.

"Daddy, this is Joe," Holly said.

Her father put out his hand for me to shake and as I grasped it I said, "It's a pleasure to meet you sir." His hand was as rough as sand paper and his grip was the grip of a man who had done a lot of hard work in his life.

"Just call me 'Red,'" her father said. "Come on in and have a sody pop."

"Okay," I said, but I just couldn't get the word 'Red' out of my mouth. It was one of those times when I was wasn't quite sure if he really wanted me to call him by his nickname or if it was a test. How can I describe 'Red?' Well, it would be safe to say that he was a genuine, 100 percent redneck, as far as I was concerned. His neck and face were craggily and sunburned, as if he had been riding the range all day, herding cattle. He wore an old straw cowboy hat, a pair of faded jeans and cowboy boots that looked like museum pieces. He walked with a bit of a limp. This guy was one tough son of a bitch, I thought. Needless to say, I was intimidated. But as it turned out, he couldn't have been nicer.

We sat and had a long, relaxed chat, during which time he told me about his life on the oil fields, working on the rigs and how he had to retire as how his legs were "nigh wore out." I let him do most of the talking because my life just didn't seem all that interesting by comparison. Finally, he turned to Holly and said, "You kids have a good time." That was it. I was approved. He never told me what time Holly had to be home or that he would beat the crap out of me if she was late. Nothing. He didn't even have a shotgun standing in the corner of the room as a subtle hint of what could happen if things went wrong. It didn't matter. He needed no such nuanced symbols of his supremacy over me. I was going to bring his only child home early and happy.

Still, you can imagine my surprise when Holly sprang that interesting bit of information on me, just at the most inopportune moment. What could I say? Did she want me to deny that I was a Mexican, or did she want to live dangerously and actually go against her parent's wishes? I couldn't tell. Finally, I tried to say something neutral, not wanting to ruin the romantic atmosphere: "Well, you know, the name 'Lewels' is German," I finally said.

"Oh," she said, "I thought maybe you were Italian."

"Whew!" I had dodged a bullet, at least for the time being. I knew that eventually she would find out somehow that I was a bit "Mexicany." We had a good time and we stayed friends, but I didn't want to take a chance that I would someday have to deal with Red when he wasn't in such a good mood, so I moved on to greener pastures, as they say.

Over the years I have been asked by many if I was Greek, Italian, or even Middle Eastern. I inherited just enough of that olive-colored skin from my grandfather, Vicente's, side of the family to allow me to pass for a number of nationalities. That, and the German last name, came in quite handy through much of my life. But if my last name had been "Cisneros," like my mother's or "Oviedo," like my father's mother, I think my life would have been much different. My family, for the most part, passed for White, Anglo-Saxon, which we were, even if we were also "Mexicany." I was, in fact, part German, part Spanish, maybe some French, and, I believe, a bit Mayan. That's not a bad combination, even if I do say so. There have been times in my life when it was more convenient to play the role of an Anglo, as in the case above, but there have also been times when being "Mexicany" worked to my advantage. I am not ashamed to say I took advantage of both versions, as the case demanded.

Even so, I had always been aware that Holly's parents weren't the only parents in town with the "no Mexicans" rule. I knew of a case in which the Anglo girl had to lie about her boyfriend's Mexican nationality, even coming up with a fake name for him. He spoke English fluently and came from a wealthy, highly-educated family in the city of Juárez. None of that seemed to matter. Ultimately, when they turned 18, they eloped. The girl's family disowned her and cut off all communication.

Racism was, and always has been in the air along the border, after all, Texans and Mexicans battled each other fiercely for the territory only a little more than 100 years before I was born. My dad described to me how Mexicans were forced to sit in the balconies in the movie theaters and ride in the back of the bus in El Paso when he was young. When he worked at the newspaper, the death of a Mexican-American was rarely deemed important, while the death of an Anglo was given large headlines. But in my youth, race relations had improved significantly, in large part to the fact that the city had become more than 60 percent Mexicany. In 1957 El Paso elected its first Mexican-American mayor, Raymond Telles, who later served as ambassador to Costa Rica, appointed by President John F. Kennedy.

Yes, things had improved markedly by the 1960s when I was in high school, yet I was glad people knew me as "Joe" Lewels and not as "Pancho" Lewels. Maybe if I had ended up going to schools on the Southside, such as Bowie or Jefferson high schools, which were almost entirely made up of Mexicany kids, I might have preferred to be called "Francisco," or maybe "Paco." But that wasn't the case. Throughout my school years I was pretty much surrounded by Anglo classmates and Anglo teachers. At Burges High in those days, the school had the reputation of being strict and having high academic standards, which in later years I appreciated. Even though I was coasting, it wasn't easy to earn a "B" average at Burges High, home of the Mustangs (the school mascot.)

Back to the topic of "getting cool" in high school, I can imagine the surprise you must have felt when I mentioned that little-miss Holly was out with one of the popular boys. That must have been a shocker. How did little, dumb, awkward, shy, inconspicuous Francisco/Joe manage to get popular when all he really wanted to do is remain average and blend in? Well, it all had to do with my sister, Helen. You see, my sister was a senior as I entered my freshman year and she had become quite a beauty and very popular, even though her real name is not "Helen"—it is "Aurora Elena," like our mother. She had done a good job of blending into Anglo society. She was voted one of the school's most popular girls when she was named Homecoming Queen that year. I was quite proud to be her little brother. People were always asking me "Is Helen Lewels your sister?" And I was always proud to say "Yes, yes she is."

Even so, I harbored no notions of becoming cool myself; I wouldn't even know how to begin. I just wanted to be one of the many, kind of like when a guy goes to prison for the first time and has to keep his head down, and be sure to not look anyone in the eye.

I wouldn't necessarily say I qualified to be considered a nerd, after all I wasn't an egghead. I didn't play in the band and I didn't sing in the choir. The cool guys played football or basketball, two sports that were out of my league due to the fact that I wasn't big enough for either one, and that I had no measurable athletic ability. I had no musical ability either. I was just average. There was one other way to be cool, and that was by belonging to one of the boy's clubs that were sanctioned by the school. There were several, but the coolest seemed to be the Mustang Club, made up mostly of athletes, while The Tangus Association, which was much smaller, was made up of a wide array of guys who couldn't easily be labeled. There were Mexicany guys and some athletes, as well as a guy who played in the band, and a few bad boys. It also had some really cool guys who were not athletes, but were just a bit mysterious. My sister told me, "If you ever join a club, make sure it's Tangus. That's the cool one."

Each club had its own distinct corduroy jackets, which made its members stand out in school and out. The Mustang Club had purple jackets, while

Tangus had white jackets. (Purple and white were the school colors.) Each had its own symbol or "coat of arms" embroidered on the back and the member's name was embroidered on the front, just above the pocket on the left side. Any guy who wore one of these jackets was automatically cool. However, as a freshman I had no hopes of ever getting into any club and even if I did, freshmen were not allowed to join. In any case, my shyness was an obstacle that would have to be overcome if I was ever to become cool.

Shyness, I now realize, is a symptom of low self-esteem. Looking back on it, I can see that my low esteem came from the fact that as a Mexicany kind of kid, I never quite felt I fit into Anglo society. I always felt I was outside looking in. Regardless of my successes in life, the feeling has always stayed with me. It has caused me to be somewhat of an introvert, even though most people don't see me that way. Another way of saying it is that due to my Mexican heritage and the fact that I was raised in an Anglo-American environment, I always felt that I was a minority of one. I expended a lot of energy just trying to fit in and hiding my secret identity. It wasn't that I was ashamed of being a Mexican, because I saw nothing shameful about it. For me it was just a matter of survival.

All of that changed in my sophomore year in 1961. On one of the first days of classes that year I happened to notice a sheet of paper that was stapled to the large bulletin board in the entry foyer of the school. It was a sign-up sheet for those boys who would like to be considered for membership in The Tangus Association. (The word "Tangus" came from reversing the syllables in "mustang" and then leaving out the "m.") I stared at it for a long time, but I didn't sign it. I figured I would have no chance. But that evening I decided to consult my sister. She was unequivocal. "Sign up!" she said. I think she didn't want to be associated with a little twirp—a nobody. So, the next day I signed the sheet. There were already more than 30 boys who had signed up.

This act of sheer audacity on my part had the effect of making me very nervous. I almost went back to erase my name. "Who was I to sign up for

Tangus?" I asked myself. I couldn't come up with a good answer. The next day the sheet had been taken down and replaced with a notice that The Tangus Association would begin interviewing applicants that Friday night at one of the member's homes at 8 p.m. sharp. Now I was really nervous. I didn't know I would have to be interviewed! Good Lord, what could I possibly have to say? I fretted all week and even considered just not showing up. But my sister wouldn't have it.

"You've gotta go," she said.

"But they're gonna interview me. What should I say?" I begged.

"Just relax and be yourself," were her final words.

But that didn't help because I didn't know who "myself" was. What did it mean to be "myself?" How would "myself" answer questions? I came to the disturbing conclusion that I had no personality whatsoever. They may as well have been asking questions to a crash dummy. I paced the floor and nearly had a nervous breakdown that week until Friday night came around. Because I didn't even have a car, I had to get my dad to drive me, leave me off a block away and wait for me. "Maybe I really was a nerd," I thought.

There were about 35 boys standing around in front of the house where the interviews were to take place and we were told to get in line and wait until our name was called. It was a long wait and with every passing moment I was getting more and more nauseated. I studied the faces of those who had gone before me as they came out. None of them were smiling. Not a good sign. Finally they called my name and I entered the living room where all the club members were plopped down on the available chairs and on the floor. At the dining room table sat the officers of the club, all facing toward the living room. There was a folding chair placed in front of the table, facing the inquisitors.

"Take a seat," someone said, pointing at the folding chair. So I did.

I sat there facing five upperclassmen, who by the fact that they were the officers of The Tangus Association, were de facto, the coolest guys in school. I felt very much out of my league. I tried to steady my nerves by breathing slowly and deeply although I felt like running out of the room and down the street to my dad.

The president of the club, a guy renowned to be the coolest guy at school, Jimmy Wingo, looked at me and asked the first question. It was a real curve ball—one that I did not anticipate.

"Why do you want to be a member of Tangus?" he asked.

"Oh my God," I thought. "I never expected that question." It sent my mind reeling with thoughts bouncing in every direction in my brain. "Should I make up a clever answer?" Should I just admit I had no reason and just get up and walk out in humiliation?"

Finally, after what seemed an eternity, I blurted out, "My sister made me do it," which was the truth.

To my amazement, this got a huge laugh from the whole room.

"So who's you're sister?" he asked.

"Helen Lewels," I answered.

"Wasn't she the Homecoming Queen last year?" he asked.

"Yes."

"And she told you to sign up for Tangus?"

"Yes," I said. "She said if I joined any other club she wouldn't speak to me again," I explained, once again telling the truth.

The room burst out in laughter once again; even my inquisitors found it funny. This had the effect of calming me down. "Laughter can't be bad," I thought. At that point some of the other officers asked me questions, but I can't remember what they were. Then I was excused. The list of new members was to be posted on the bulletin board on Monday morning, I was told. As I walked out I felt proud of myself for not puking in front of them or for not curling up into a ball on the floor and having to be carried out. It had gone much better than I had expected, but I still didn't think I would be chosen. After all, what kind of an answer was "my sister told me to?" I thought that was pretty lame. In retrospect, I thought I should have been able to foresee they would ask that question. If I had, then I could have been prepared with a more well-thought out answer, such as: "I believe that becoming a member of The Tangus Association will make me a better student and a better citizen of my community." Or, "I hear Tangus has bitchin' keg parties." I was sure I could have come up with something better than "my sister made me do it." Darn, if I had only known ahead of time.

I took the bus to school on Monday as usual, along with all the other nerds, and went straight to the bulletin board. Nothing. There was no announcement posted yet, so I waited. I hung back, down the hall a bit, but still within eyesight of the board. But finally the bell rang and I had to get to first period class. After class I ran back to check. Still nothing. And so it went all day. By then I was certain I had no chance. "Maybe this year's recruits were so bad they wouldn't let anyone in," I thought.

But just after the fifth period of the day I ran by the board to check once more and to my amazement, there it was. It said: "The Tangus Association is happy to announce its new members." There were five names on the list. The fifth one was "Joe Lewels." I nearly fainted. "Oh God," I thought. "What do I do now? Am I supposed to act differently? Should I run around telling everyone I know?" No, I reasoned, that would not be cool. The cool thing to do is to act nonchalant, as if it were not a big deal. So I went to sixth-period class and didn't say a word about it. I was beginning to see what it meant to be cool. Being cool was all about not acting cool. It was about really being cool. But inside, I wanted to jump with joy. And I couldn't wait to get my white Tangus jacket. Whooppee! I was cool!

The next day was an altogether different kind of day for me. I didn't have to say anything to anyone because everyone came up to me throughout the day to congratulate me. I had friends I didn't know I had. Cute girls particularly took an interest in me, even some of the upper-class ones. Then, one by one, the members of Tangus made a point of stopping me in the halls to shake my hand in congratulations, as if we were all members of some sacred and secret society. I was told our first meeting was to be held the following Friday night at an undisclosed location. One of the members would come by my house to pick me up. In the meantime I was to go to the place that makes the jackets to be fitted for one and to have my name embroidered on the front.

That Friday I told my parents I had to attend my first Tangus meeting and I wasn't sure what time I would be home. They seemed okay with that. When my ride came, I asked where we were going, but he said he couldn't say, but we were heading downtown. When we got downtown, we drove over the bridge to Juárez and parked down the street from a bar called, *El Submarino*, which means, "The Submarine." I almost said that I wasn't allowed to go to Juárez, but I held back because even I knew that would not be cool. We walked down the stairs to the dimly-lit basement where there was a long bar with about 20 bar stools. Most of them were already taken by the members. They came up and congratulated me and the other new members and explained that the club met here once a month. And then it was time to sit at the bar and order three tequila shots, five cents apiece. I was 15 years old and had never had a whole drink, but what could I do? We all proceeded to down our three shots and then we made our way to "Fred's Rainbow Bar," where we would have plenty of space to have a beer and get to know one another. "Boy," I thought, "Tangus is a lot cooler than I had ever thought."

That night the new guys were indoctrinated in Tangus lore. We were let in on some of the mysteries that surrounded the organization, some of which I still cannot reveal. However, there was one secret at the core of the organization that we talked about—the fabled and mystical "Zodiac" room—a secret location where most of the club meetings were held and where only Tangus members were permitted to enter. That was where we would have our next meeting—no girls allowed, ever!

It was late when I was dropped off in front of my house and I was feeling quite dizzy. I was hoping to get to my room without seeing anyone, but my parents were still up watching TV so I had to walk by them on the way to my room. "How was your meeting?" my mother asked? "Tell us about it."

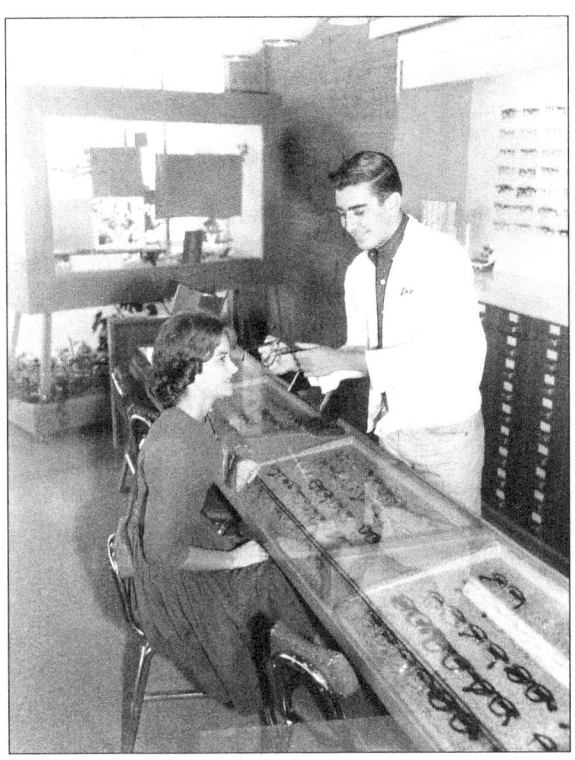

Last known picture of the famous Tangus jacket, senior year at Burges High School (1962).

"It was okay," I managed to say, and then I marched past them as straight as I could and into my room. I think I got away with it, but I didn't get away without a really bad headache all the next day. Getting cool, it seems, has its price.

By the time the meeting day rolled around, I had experienced being cool for almost three weeks and the transformation from nerdy to popular was nothing short of miraculous. What had in the past been seen as shyness and lack of self-confidence by others, now took on the appearance of being mysterious and a bit dark—maybe even sensitive. The Tangus jacket made all the difference. As I walked the halls of Burges, I noticed girls who would normally not give me a second look, passing me with broad smiles. They were actually making eye contact with me, something I had never experienced. Even the guys were coming up and trying to be chummy. I handled the attention by remaining shy and quiet, which only enhanced my popularity. I was suddenly being nominated for various honors—student council representative was first, and the next year I became vice-president of the junior class. As a senior, I was voted assistant editor of the school newspaper. Who would have thought?

The final initiation into Tangus was to be held at the "Zodiac" on Friday night and attendance was mandatory. Tangus was a small club of only 25 or so boys, while the Mustang club was huge—possibly 100 boys. This gave the appearance that Tangus was much more exclusive, therefore, cooler. I arrived a bit early for the meeting and there were already a few members, all wearing their jackets, standing out in front of a house in El Paso's lower valley. Apparently the "Zodiac" was behind the house and no one was allowed in until the meeting was to start. There was a certain electricity in the air in expectation of finally being admitted into the sacrosanct chamber reserved only for members.

Finally, the president of the club came out and ushered us to the back of the house where we saw a free-standing building about the size of a two-car garage with a door on one side. I'll never forget the sight that I beheld as I walked in. The room was furnished only with mattresses and mats on the floor and the dim, red lighting filled the room with a sense of foreboding. The walls were splattered with swaths of different colored paints—red, black, and dark blue. If you squinted your eyes, you could just make out patterns and symbols. There was a black light up above that made our white jackets glow. It was the most mysterious place I had ever seen.

The meeting was called to order and the president introduced the new members and we were all sworn to maintain strict confidence about where the "Zodiac" was and about anything that occurred therein. Then, the sergeant at arms, Jack Caldarella, took the floor, literally. He was to make a speech or an announcement, it wasn't clear. All eyes were on Jack, a popular football player and basketball letterman, who sat on a mat by the door. For his address, he chose to lie down on his back, which I thought odd. Then, he raised his legs high in the air and spread them wide, which I thought quite strange. Then, out of nowhere he pulled out a cigarette lighter, and placed it firmly against the seat of his pants. "What the heck?" I thought. Then he lit the lighter and, after a few tense moments, he farted a two-foot-long, blue flame high into the air. It was the most amazing thing I had ever seen. I knew at that moment that I had reached the epitomé of coolness. The room broke out into hoots and hollers, and wild applause, for we all knew the meaning of that display. We were all now true members of that secret and ever-so-cool club—The Tangus Association. I was in awe and I had to catch my breath, literally.

I still get teary-eyed whenever I think of that moment. That fart changed my life.

ON the RIO GRANDE

10

Chapter *Diez*
California Dreamin

As you may recall, my mom went to great trouble to help me enroll at Texas Western College (TWC)—(Go Miners!) in the fall of 1962. It wasn't that I really wanted to go to college...yet. In fact, I had been thinking I might just take a year off from the rigors of trying to get smart and run off to the beaches of Southern California for a year or so to mull over the possibilities. The Beach Boys songs had become popular by then, and they beckoned teens by the many thousands to the warm, sandy, bikini-strewn beaches of our Western shores. They were the pied pipers of their time, luring young people to the land of eternal beach parties where they could smoke and drink and...oh oh! Pinocchio! I forgot.

You see, my parents hadn't talked to us kids about college. There was no dinner-table talk about which ones offered the best programs or the importance of scoring high on entrance exams. There were no lectures about how I should become a doctor or a lawyer or a businessman. My parents didn't have a clue about what it would take to get into college or what it would cost. I pretty much exceeded their greatest expectations when I graduated from elementary school. That was more than either of them had ever accomplished. Beyond that, they had no specific plans for me. I was never pushed to get good grades or even to do my homework. By the time my sister and I graduated from high school, my parents were already in awe of us and assumed we could accomplish anything. As for my sister, she chose to get married and raise a family.

In my case, my parent's laissez-faire attitude toward my future had the effect of causing me to just coast through high school, and never consider the possibility of getting a scholarship to a good school. I seriously had not thought the issue through, but then the great day of reckoning arrived: graduation. It happened so suddenly that when it arrived I had no idea what I was to do. I thought I could get a job, but I had no prospects. It was one of those times in life when you find yourself with nothing to do, nowhere to go, and no money to do it with. I was adrift at sea without a paddle. Then, two of my friends (Rudy and Jimmy) came by the house and announced their great plan. They were going to California for the summer and they wanted me to go with them. "I don't have any money," I said, wistfully.

"You don't need much," my friend, Rudy, said. "We can take my station wagon, pack some bed rolls and load up on canned food and cereal boxes from our houses."

"Well, we still need money," I said.

"Jimmy and I each have seventy-five dollars," Rudy said. I bet your dad would give you that much. We can camp out along the way and when we get there we can crash with some friends of mine who have an apartment near the beach."

I'm not sure how or why, but my dad gave me the money; I ransacked our kitchen cupboard and filled two cardboard boxes with canned food; I packed a bag and we left the next day. It seems that I had completely forgotten the important lessons that Pinocchio had taught me as child. I was headed straight for that dreaded amusement park where kids are turned into donkeys.

It had the innocent-sounding name of "Los Angeles," which in Spanish means "The Angels." But heck, why not?

As we were leaving El Paso, Rudy decided to make a little detour (a 90 degree turn) and head for Denver where we had a friend (Ron) who would put us up. Ron's parents had a basement where we crashed, and at dinner his father said, "How would you boys like to make a little money?" It turned out he owned a construction company and he had the need for men to clean off scaffolding for a new job. He was willing to pay us each $5 an hour. We looked at each other and decided we were in. So the next day we went to work and by the time we left Denver the following week, we each had an extra $250 dollars. Can life get any easier?

As we left Denver after partying heartily, we realized we would be passing through Las Vegas on the way to L.A. Jimmy said, "Hey I have an uncle in Vegas. I haven't seen him for years, but he might let us stay with him. I'll call him when we get there." When we arrived Jimmy called his long-lost Uncle Jack, who seemed overjoyed to hear from Jimmy. "So what did he say?" we asked as he stepped out of the phone booth.

"He said to meet him at some hotel called the Stardust," Jimmy replied. "He said we couldn't miss it because it's on the strip. I guess he works there. And he wants us to go over to his house for dinner."

"Well, we can't disappoint your good old uncle Jack, now, can we?" Rudy said. We all agreed that a home-cooked meal was a lot better than a can of beans warmed over a campfire. So off we went.

Arriving to Las Vegas at night for the first time as a teenage boy was like arriving at the Pearly Gates of heaven. The bright lights were astonishing, and as we drove down the street with our windows open we could hear the sounds of the slot machines paying out their jackpots and the gamblers shouting and laughing. We couldn't wait to get into the casinos and hit it big like all the other tourists. But suddenly it hit me. Las Vegas was just like the pleasure palace that Pinocchio was taken to by the hooligans! Yikes! I knew I had to be careful, but then I thought, "Just how much trouble can we get into in one night? No sweat; everything will be fine."

Uncle Jack was right, the Stardust Hotel and Casino was impossible to miss. It was huge—one of the biggest in Vegas at the time. We pulled into the covered entrance and a valet took the keys to the beat-up station wagon as if we were famous movie stars. Uncle Jack was standing there waiting for us as promised. It turned out he was the bell captain at the hotel, which we later learned is a huge deal in Las Vegas.

"Hi, boys!" he shouted as he embraced Jimmy. "Welcome to Las Vegas. I've got a room reserved for you. When we get from dinner you can move your stuff in. Stay as long as you want. It's on me!"

Do things like this really happen to teenagers on a road trip? Well, they did to us that summer of 1962. I couldn't make this up if I wanted to!

With that, a valet pulled up in a brand-new, red Cadillac convertible, which Uncle Jack later explained had belonged to a former high roller who lost everything and had to sell his car fast. Uncle Jack said he got a great deal. It was clear that the job of head bellman was a lucrative position, and one that had many advantages, some of which I'm not sure I should write about.

In any case, yada-yada-yada, we spent a week lounging by the pool, ordering our meals from room service (on the house) and, as we were underage, sneaking into the casinos to play the nickel slots. It didn't cost us a penny, just a few nickels. Vegas was great, but it wasn't the beach. So after a week, we said thank you and goodbye to Uncle Jack and headed west. We could already smell the sweet, salt air of the Pacific Ocean, and we weren't in the mood for any more detours. "The Beach Boy's" songs were buzzing in our heads.

Songs like "Surfin' Safari:"
"Let's go surfin' now,
Everybody's learning how, come on a safari with me."
And "Little Surfer Girl:"
"I have watched you on the shore,
Standing by the ocean roar,

Do you love me, do you surfer girl?"

And "California Girls":

"I've been all around this great big world and I've seen all kinds of girls, yeah, but I couldn't wait to get back in the states, back to the cutest in the states. I wish they all could be California girls."

Unbelievably, we got to Los Angeles with money to burn. For the next two months or so, we slept in bedrolls on the floors of various friend's and near-friend's apartments, went to parties, met girls and checked out all the surfing beaches in the area. At night we would make a bonfire on the beach and California kids would show up ready to party. Someone always had a radio, so, just like in the movies, we danced the "Twist," the "Watusi," and the "Mashed Potato," and we partied late into the night. Sometimes we would just sleep on the beach 'til dawn. How could life get any better than this?

Somehow the meager supplies and little cash we started with had gotten us through our winding journey. By the time the "endless" summer was finally over our money was getting a little low and the draft board was sending out "greeting cards" to all eligible young men. And that meant us.

No one I knew was inclined to join the Army or go to war, but it wasn't a choice. We were going to get drafted unless we did something drastic like run off to Canada or enroll in college. As long as we were full-time college students the draft would give us a deferment. That was the rule. Since Canada was far too cold and too far away for me, I chose college. My life of leisure had come to an end. I hitched a ride home with another friend from El Paso because Rudy and Jimmy were having too much fun to leave; they stayed and waited for the draft board to call. When I got home, I accompanied my mother to the pawn shop to get my tuition money and that was that. I was going to college, the only one we could afford. TWC was a state school and it was required to accept any fool/applicant who had a diploma from any Texas high school, no matter how dumb he was. I was in luck!

Looking back on my life, I can see how so much of it was influenced by the Vietnam War. If it hadn't been for the draft, I might not have ever gone to college. The draft was a powerful force that propelled me and many of my friends to not only go to college, but to study and keep our grades up. Those who flunked out were getting drafted and sent to Vietnam. I had to renew the vows I made in the second grade to start getting smart. I realized I hadn't done a very good job so far, but there was still time. I had a second chance and I was going to make the most of it. I was going to get a job, pay for my tuition and study like mad. That was when I met my friend Gary Miller.

11

Chapter Once
Old Gringo

Gary and I met in class on the first day of college and we hit it off right away. Gary was a pure gringo from a little Texas town called "Big Lake," a few hundred miles to the southeast. He actually thought he was from West Texas until he got to El Paso, which is so far west it is all but forgotten by the rest of Texas. El Paso, wedged tightly between Old Mexico and New Mexico, seemed like another world to him. Whereas he was from the flatlands, El Paso's Mount Franklin divides the city in half and tops out at over 7,000 feet. The Rio Grande River, which cuts right through downtown, serves as the Mexican border, winding its way for more than 700 miles all the way to the Gulf of Mexico. Gary discovered quickly that El Paso bore no resemblance at all to his hometown and he loved every bit of it. He was eager to learn as much as he could about life on the border and particularly, life across the border.

Well, he could not have found a better guide. As you know, in high school, my friends and I had gotten to know the city of Juárez intimately.

The bartenders on the other side of the river didn't care how old the patrons were. If you could sit on the stool, and if you had dollars, you would be served. Drinks were cheap. Real cheap. We would order shots of tequila for five cents at some of the sleazier bars, and a beer was only a quarter in most places.

On weekends we would go to the Lobby Bar, listen to live music and find girls to dance with. Gary couldn't get enough of it. He might as well have been at Disneyland.

Many school days we would drive over the bridge, park on a side street and have lunch at Fred's Rainbow Bar, our favorite hangout. A cold "Cruz Blanca" beer, a sandwich and chips would cost us 75 cents. With another quarter we would feed the juke box and play Ray Charles' "Born to Lose" over and over again. I don't know why. How could you beat those prices? After lunch we would go down the street to Hugos billiard parlor and play a few games of pool. We still made it back across the border in time to go to work because in those days there weren't long lines at the bridge. Juárez might just as well have been merely an extension of downtown El Paso.

One of the first things I had to explain to Gary after crossing over the bridge was the new traffic rules he would have to get used to. This was after he said, "Gee it doesn't look like people stop at 'stop' signs over here or at red lights. This is crazy."

"Well, "I explained, "you just need to know the rules."

"What rules?

"The first rule is don't get into a traffic accident over here because you might not see your car for a while. It'll get impounded and you might have to pay a "mordida," (a bite).

"What's a mordida? He asked.

"It's kind of like a fine, but you just pay it directly to the policeman. It's negotiable."

"Negotiable? I don't get it."

"It depends on how much the policeman can get out of you. If you look wealthy, it costs more. If he sees a wad of bills when you open your wallet to show your ID, the fine will go up. If you're broke, it might cost you ten bucks. So always look broke when you come over here."

"Well, that won't be a problem for me."

"There's a couple more rules," I volunteered. "First is, gringos pay more, so try to look bit Mexicany and brush up on your Spanish."

Gary just looked at me with a skeptical glare. "Yeah, I'll try to do that," he said sarcastically.

"No, really," I said. "I'll help you with your Spanish. There are a few phrases that will come in handy. For example, when you are with your Mexicany girlfriend, you can tell her, "*Te amo mucho.*" That means you love her a lot. Or you can say, "*Béseme culo,*" which means "Kiss me a lot."

He was able to repeat these phrases to my satisfaction, so we went on to another important lesson. "Another thing that is real important is when you are with a group of people at a bar or restaurant, you have to tell the waiter or bartender, '*La cuenta es para mi amigo*' and then point to someone."

"Oh yeah?" Gary asked a bit suspiciously. "What does that mean?"

"That means, 'The tab is for my friend.' Just say that to the waiter when you're about to leave and then excuse yourself and go to the men's room for a few minutes. Works every time."

"Oh that's a good one, I'll definitely remember that one," Gary said laughingly.

"There is one more traffic rule you need to know, "I said. "It's called the ROL."

"What's the ROL?"

"That's the rule for when you're stuck in a traffic jam. All you do if you want to change lanes is jam in front of the guy next to you so that your bumper is in front of his bumper. Then you have the right of way. It's called the "Rule of Overlap."

"That's crazy," Gary said. "That's a good way to get into a fight."

"No, it really works," I explained. You see everyone is so afraid of having to deal with a cop and pay a mordida that they will stop before bumping into you. Isn't that great?"

"Yeah, I'll be sure to try that the next time I drive over here," he answered sarcastically.

"Well," I said, "as long as you follow my instructions, you'll stay out of trouble," I said reassuringly.

Gary did try to follow my instructions, but sometimes trouble can find you even when you aren't looking for it. One day Gary arrived at school with a black eye, cuts on his face and his right hand was bandaged. "Gary," I asked, "what in the world happened to you?"

"Awww," he said in his Texas twang, "It's no big di'l."

"It looks like a big deal to me! Were you in a car wreck?" I asked.

"Naw," he said, "I just got into a little tussle."

"A little tussle? It looks like it was a big tussle," I said. "Tell me what happened."

"Well, last night around ten o'clock I got hungry for some tacos, so I drove down to 'Chicos' down on Alameda Street. When I came out, some 'cholos' jumped me. (The term 'cholos' refers to 'Mexicany' gang-type young men.) Gary had inadvertently strayed into their territory. "How many were there?" I asked.

"Four," he replied briefly. Since Gary was not a man of many words and he rarely overstated anything, I believed him. (I think his quiet, but strong nature is what caused the Central Intelligence Agency (CIA) to recruit him later in life. When the FBI was doing his background check they came to interview me, as Gary had listed me as a reference. I explained to them that he was the kind of guy who could keep a secret, even after a few shots of tequila. I think they liked that because he was hired by the CIA shortly thereafter.)

"Four guys jumped you?" I asked in wonderment. "So what happened next?" I asked, but I could have guessed. You see, had the four young men known what I knew about Gary Miller, they would have just gone the other way. They made a big mistake by underestimating this gringo. As I have already noted, Gary grew up in the oilfields and worked on the oil rigs each summer. He saved his money for his college education. In case you are not aware of this fact, oil-rig workers are tough. It is hard work—so hard that most young men would not last a day. I know I wouldn't have. But Gary was one tough son of a bitch. He didn't look it because he wasn't big. He was about 5'9" and weighed about 160 pounds. His blond hair was already thinning, so he wore it in a slight comb-over, making him look older than he was. And he wore glasses. He must have looked like an easy mark. But what you couldn't tell by looking at him was that he was solid muscle. When he wasn't on an oil rig, he was playing football for his high school team. Gary and a group of our friends had started working out with weights at the YMCA in our spare time and I was amazed that he could bench press nearly 200 pounds.

I already knew how this story was going to end.

"Well," he said, laughingly, "they were all over me in a second and I just started punchin'. It didn't matter where I aimed because they were all around me. I just kept my head down and kept punchin' 'til it was over. Then the cops showed up. They were going to arrest me!" he said in disbelief.

"You?" I asked. "What about the other guys?"

"Well, they had to go to the hospital. That's why the cops were going to arrest me."

"You mean all four of them went to the hospital?" I asked unbelievingly.

"Well, I didn't stop swinging until they did. By the time it was over they were all on the ground. That's when the cops came," he said. "It took me a while to convince them I didn't start the fight and I was just defending myself. Once they realized what happened, they let me go."

"Damn," I said admiringly. "They picked on the wrong gringo didn't they?" I laughed.

"Yeah, I guess so," he stated bluntly. "Let's go to class."

The more I got to know about Gary, the more I liked him. He would never start a fight. It just wasn't in his nature. He was a sweet, funny and smart guy. What was not to like?

In our sophomore year Gary asked me to go home with him to Big Lake (about 50 miles southeast of Midland) for spring break so I could meet his family and he could show me around. I eagerly accepted the invitation as I was excited about going to the lake, something we lacked in the high desert of El Paso. We packed our bags, a couple of cases of Coors beer for his buddies back home, and some sandwiches. Then we jumped into his old MG car, and we were off. I wasn't really sure where Big Lake was then, but during the long drive Gary regaled me with many stories about what it was like to grow up in a small town. He told me about his friends and his girlfriends and many of the antics he was involved in during his high-school years. Half way there I felt I was getting to know the town intimately. Gary described it as a small town in the West Texas oilfields—the flat lands of the Great Plains. I had never been anywhere else in Texas so it sounded remotely exotic. I knew it had a drive-in theater and a traffic light, but that the only movie theater in town had closed. I couldn't wait to see it all. And then he casually dropped a bombshell. "Oh yeah," I forgot to tell you about my airplane."

"You have an airplane?" I asked unbelievingly. It was just like Gary not to mention the most important thing.

"Well, it's not just mine," he answered, "It belongs to our flying club."

"Wow," I responded. "That is really cool!" I couldn't wait to see it. I also had an interest in flying at that time. In fact, in our junior year I was going to start learning to fly myself—a fact that had impressed Gary to no end.

"Well, maybe we can go for a ride in it," I said excitedly.

"Naw, I don't think we can do that. It needs a little work. But we can go see it," he said.

"Okay," I said disappointedly. "But when are we going to the lake?" I asked.

"What lake?" Gary asked.

"The lake," I said. "You know, 'Big Lake'. I brought my swim suit."

"There's no lake." he said laughingly. He thought it was the funniest joke he ever heard. "You really packed a swim suit?" he asked, unbelievingly.

"What do you mean there's no lake? Why do they call it 'Big Lake'?" I asked, feeling a bit betrayed. I had really been looking forward to seeing the big lake and maybe doing a little boating and water skiing.

"Well maybe there used to be a lake once—millions of years ago." He laughed. "Now the lake is underground. It's a lake of "awl." That's why there's so many "awl"rigs." He couldn't stop laughing. I, on the other hand, was sorely disappointed. A town called "Big Lake," that has no lake. Who would have thought? I stewed on that for a while and in my disappointment I said. "You know, Gary, if you're going to make it in American society you're going to have to learn to speak proper American!"

Gary thought this hilarious—a Mexicany guy was going to teach him how to speak English. "What are you talking about?" he laughed.

"In the first place, when you saw my friend's motorcycle, you called it a 'motorsickle'. The word is 'cycle', like 'sigh-kel'" I said, emphasizing the 'sigh.'

"Oh, that's no big di'l" he said.

I said, "The word is 'deal' not 'd'il'"

"Okay, okay," he protested. I get it."

But I was just getting started. I had decided to make Gary my pet project. I was going to take the "hick" out of him and help him become a real American, not an "Amerkin."

"Okay, here's another example, I said. Take the word 'oil.' A minute ago you said there was a lake of 'awl' underground. Now as a college man you should know that 'awl' is not a word. The word is 'O I L,' and it's pronounced 'oh-IL,' not 'awl.' You're leaving out the 'I,'" I said sternly.

He just thought that was the funniest thing he had ever heard and he couldn't stop laughing. He had grown up in the "awl" fields and yet, here was a city boy trying to teach him how to say the word correctly. But I wasn't finished. "Also, since we are on the subject of teaching you to speak American, tell me what this is," I ordered as I held up my left hand with my middle finger extended. This really made him laugh. "I'm not kidding, Gary, tell me what this is." I demanded.

When he was able to stop laughing, he said, "That's a 'fanger.'"

"No!" I said emphatically, "This is not a 'fanger.' It's a FINGER! F-I-N-G-E-R. There is no 'A' in the word 'finger.' Now he was really laughing. It was as if he had never noticed that the word 'finger' was spelled with an 'I' instead of with an 'A.' "Now say it," I ordered. "FINGER." It's easy, the first part is like the word 'ring,' you can say that can't you?"

"Yeah, yeah," he said, still laughing. "Fiiiing-er, fiiing-er," he repeated, mockingly.

"You see," I said. "That's not so difficult, is it? And while we are on the subject, you also say 'thang,' instead of 'thing.' I lectured. If you don't learn to speak proper English, people will think you're just a dumb hick instead of a college-educated, intellectual. More importantly, you will totally strike out with the chicks."

"Okay, okay, I get it. You have a point." he said. "You're right. I'll work on it."

"By the way," I said, "how is it going with that cute Mexican girl you're dating, Nina. Have you tried out the Spanish I taught you?"

"Oh yeah," he replied, "I've been meaning to talk to you about that. She kind of liked it when I told her '*Te amo mucho*,' but she got a big kick out of the other phrase, 'Béseme culo.' She said it didn't mean 'kiss me a lot.' She said it means 'kiss my ass.' Thanks a lot."

"Well," I said, "I guess it could be subject to interpretation."

"Interpretation my ass," he replied.

"Well you said she thought it was funny, right?"

"Yeah, we both laughed a lot. She's got a good sense of humor."

"So it sounds like it's going well with her." I probed.

"No, not so well. Her folks don't like her dating gringos, so we're going to have to break up or just sneak around, which she doesn't want to do."

"Sounds like reverse discrimination to me," I said.

"Yeah, who would've thought?" he said, shaking his head.

By then we were driving past the drive-in theater and about to make our way into the center of town. Gary couldn't wait for me to see the traffic light. So, to change the subject, I asked, "So what other sports did you play in high school besides football?"

"Oh not much," he answered. "Just a little 'rasslin.'"

ON the RIO GRANDE

12

Chapter *Doce*
Flying 'Solo'

The highlight of the visit to Big Lake (seeing as how there wasn't any lake or movie theater, just mostly "awl" wells as far as the eye could see) was the visit to the airfield to see the airplane. There was a small airstrip just outside of what there was of a town, and there were a few old rusty hangars lined up beside it. We got out of the car and Gary pushed open the hangar door with some effort, as if it hadn't been used for quite a while. Dust and cobwebs flew everywhere. It was dark inside, so it took a while for my eyes to adjust. When I could focus clearly, I couldn't believe my eyes. "This can't be the airplane he was talking about," I thought. It was the biggest heap of junk I'd ever seen. The old, decrepit Piper Cub had a missing propeller and the skin was peeling off the frame. There were engine parts scattered about on an old table and the plane's tires were flat and bald.

"Well, like I said, it needs some work." Gary said.

All I could come up with was, "You actually flew this?"

"Oh sure. But it's been a while."

"Gary, this crate doesn't look like it's flown since World War II. I can't believe you risked your life in this heap!"

"We had her fixed up pretty good a couple a years ago. We had an old crop-duster pilot show us how to fly it. It was great." Gary said enthusiastically.

"Well, I don't think she's ever going to get airborne again." I said, shaking my head. "And even if you fixed her up, I wouldn't recommend going up in her anymore. She's had it."

"Yeah, well, it was fun while it lasted," Gary replied resignedly.

Changing the subject, Gary asked, "When do you start your flying lessons?"

Gary and I had talked about my acceptance into the Reserve Officer Training Corps (ROTC) flight program on the trip down to Big Lake. I think he was more excited about it than I was.

"Next year." I replied. "First I have to complete ground school and then we start flying." Southwest Air Rangers at the El Paso International Airport had the contract to train three ROTC cadets. If we completed the course we would get our private pilot licenses, preparing us for becoming Army aviators once we graduated from college. First we would have to successfully complete a solo flight around the airport and the final test would be a solo cross-country flight to the Midland-Odessa airport and back, about 300 miles one way.

"I have a 'gran idiota'," Gary said, using a phrase I had taught him. "I've been thinking about this for a while. I want to go with you on your cross-country flight."

"Gary, you know that phrase doesn't mean 'great idea,' don't you?" I was feeling a bit sorry for him. "It means 'big idiot."

"Oh great, I've been using it everywhere. Thanks again."

"Your big idea sounds great except it is supposed to be a 'solo' flight, and I can't take passengers until I have a license," I added.

Apparently Gary had already thought this through. "Yeah, but no one will know, and besides I know how to fly an airplane," he explained, as if that would make a difference. He hadn't actually gotten his pilot's license.

I was starting to feel guilty about misleading him with my Spanish lesson, so I said, "Okay, tell me about the part where no one would know."

"That's easy," he said. "After you take off you can fly down to the Fabens airport and pick me up, then you can drop me off on the way back," he replied. "There's no tower in Fabens. Anyone can land and take off without anybody finding out," he added. Fabens was a small town just southeast of El Paso and so it would be more-or-less on the way to Midland-Odessa. He had it all planned out.

"So, you would drive down to Fabens and leave your car, then I would drop you off on the way back to El Paso?" I asked seeking clarification.

"Exactly!" Gary said excitedly. "No one will ever know. It'll be a lot of fun."

"Well, it would be a lot more fun, if I didn't get caught," I said, warming slightly to the idea. "I'm going to have to think about it."

"Great," Gary said, as if it was a done deal. I think he knew he could count on me to have an outrageous adventure that could go insanely wrong.

"After all," I thought, "even if I get caught it won't be the end of the world. So what if I get booted out of the flight program. What are they going to do, send me to Vietnam?" I wasn't sure I even wanted to be an army pilot anyway. After all, I had put in my bid to enter the Intelligence Corps or the Signal Corps upon graduation. My third choice on the form all ROTC cadets had to complete before graduation was the Transportation Corps. Yes, the army gave us three choices for which branch suited our skills the best. I thought that was very thoughtful of them. (There are many other branches of the army I could have chosen from, such as the Infantry Corps or the Artillery Corps, but those required actually fighting on the ground, something I didn't relish.) No, army intelligence was where I wanted to be and I thought myself to be fully qualified. After all, how intelligent do you have to be to qualify? The words "army" and "intelligence" didn't even seem to go together. I thought they were actually incompatible. However, I felt certain the army was intelligent enough to honor my first choice when the time came.

There was also a difficult decision to make before signing up for flight school; I would have to serve a third year of active duty because the army flight training program was nine-months long. I would really have to think about that when the time came. Getting my private pilot's license at the expense of the army didn't require me to go to army flight school, but it would give me an option later on. For now, I was just having fun learning to fly an airplane for free, and I couldn't wait for my first solo cross country trip.

Finally, the day arrived. Our secret mission had been hatched and planned well. Gary left for Fabens early that morning and I received my final instructions from my very stern flight instructor, Mr. Zeiss. He was a lean, mean, no-nonsense German who was retired military (maybe from the Luftwaffe, I thought.) He had single-handedly cracked the whip, got me through ground school and nervously taught me the basics of flying an airplane. He was not the type to joke around or to enjoy the pleasures of flight. He took flying very seriously and seemed to fear that each and every time we took off some horrible disaster would befall us.

As we would fly over the vast desert surrounding our fair city, Mr. Zeiss delighted in suddenly pulling back the power and yelling "ENGINE FAILURE!" at the top of his lungs. That was my command to gently glide the plane down to a presumptive landing area, such as an old road or a farmer's field. The idea was that a pilot should always be on the alert, expecting a disaster at any moment and scanning the ground for potential landing areas. This really took a lot of the fun out of flying for me. Flying an airplane for Mr. Zeiss was hard work—a stressful exertion of every bodily sense. My idea of flying was that it should be joyful and serene, enjoying the sights and being one with nature, like an eagle. That was what I had in mind.

During these "forced landings," as the airplane was just about to crash into the ground, he would yell, "GO AROUND," in my ear and I had to give the plane full power to avoid crashing into the cactus-strewn sand dunes. Then he would go on a rant, endlessly critiquing my choice of landing area, complaining that I had chosen to land downwind (which is a bad "no no"), or on top of a barn, or that I had missed seeing a small landing strip only a mile in the other direction. I knew I needed to be more attentive, but there was just no pleasing him. He never smiled and rarely had any praise for my performance. Worse, knowing that an "emergency" could happen at any moment, made learning to fly much more stressful than I had imagined. I developed "jangled nerves" syndrome. I thought to myself he needed to chill out and learn to relax. After all, I wasn't going to crash the airplane. I had a qualified instructor at my side.

On the big day Mr. Zeiss said in his most official tone. "Let me see your flight plan."

I handed him my plan to fly directly to the Midland-Odessa airport, land, sign in, take off and return directly to the El Paso airport. I would follow the highway, which stretched straight as an arrow across the endless desert, and land at the Midland-Odessa airport. (How hard could that be?) The plan included the time of departure, estimated flying time, time of arrival in Midland-Odessa and the time allotted for landing, signing in and taking a short break. My time of arrival back in El Paso had been calculated with extreme care, just as Mr. Zeiss had taught us.

"Okay, Looks good," he said cautiously as he went over my map and my flight plan. "You check the weather?"

"Yes sir, looks clear. Good flying weather," I said, trying to sound efficient and upbeat, and also trying not to arouse suspicion.

"Well, okay get going. I'll be here when you get back for your debriefing."

"Yes sir," I said, wanting to click my heels together and salute.

The time had come. After doing the pre-flight check, I boarded the single-engine Piper, started it up and called the tower for taxi instructions. My life as a pilot had begun.

It was going to be a great day!

Gary was already standing at the end of the runway at the Fabens airport, as always with a huge grin on his face. He leaped in, buckled up and we were off on our greatest adventure yet. "Okay," I explained, "we're just going to follow the highway, land at the airport and take a ten-minute break. Then we'll head back. My instructor will be waiting for me, so we have to stay on schedule. Easy peasy," I added.

"Can I fly it?" Gary asked, without even saying "hello."

"Hmmm," I hesitated. "I don't know. I hadn't thought of that."

"Aw come on," Gary insisted. "Even I can follow a highway, even if I don't have a license."

"Well, you're right there," I said. "It's not like flying an airplane is any different from driving a car." "And," I thought to myself, "there's not even any traffic out here to worry about." So, once we were on our (my) course heading and at our (my) assigned altitude, I said, "Okay, take over."

He took the controls as if he were a little kid driving a bumper car for the first time. "This is great," he said. "I'm gonna get me one of these someday."

"If you like flying so much, why don't you sign up for ROTC and get into the flight program like me?" I asked.

"You see these," Gary replied, pointing to his glasses. "I would love to be an army pilot, but you have to have 20/20 vision, so I wouldn't qualify," he said with a disappointed look on his face.

"Oh, yeah," I said. "I forgot about that. So why not just sign up for ROTC and get a commission when you graduate. It would be better to go in as an officer than a grunt." I advised.

"Naw, I've decided to join the marines when I graduate," he said.

"Oh I see," I said. "That's your way of outsmarting the draft. That makes a lot of sense." Gary had a good laugh at this insight.

"Well, my older brother was a marine and he would be disappointed if I went into the army," he explained.

I couldn't believe he was serious. None of my friends had any interest in being in the military or going to fight in Vietnam. There was no overwhelming sense of patriotism for this war as there had been for the World Wars. We didn't know where Vietnam was or why we were even over there. If it hadn't been for the draft, none of us would have served in the military. Some of my friends found a loophole in the draft law. They got their girlfriends pregnant and got married (sometimes unintentionally). Married men with children were exempt. Others had allergies or some other physical disability, such as being flat footed. One of my friends had a serious, genetic spinal condition which caused him to suffer chronic pain. His doctor wrote a letter to the draft board explaining why he would not be able to serve. At his meeting with the draft board, they read the letter, wadded it up and threw it in the waste basket. He was assigned to the artillery.

My friend Rudy Terrazas, who I mentioned earlier, chose to join the Navy to avoid the draft. He was about to be sent to Vietnam when he discovered he could avoid it by volunteering to serve in the Antarctica for a year. He spent the year in semi-darkness, under the ice where there was not much to do and, worse, no attractive women. That tour of duty left him suffering from a kind of deep depression. It had been a brutal year that he said was as bad as being in prison. When his tour was over, the Navy sent him to Vietnam.

In any case, because of the war in South Vietnam, here we were, Gary and I having the time of our lives flying an airplane for free; there was nothing to do but enjoy the ride. I pushed my seat back, kicked back, relaxed and enjoyed the scenery. As we left the Franklin Mountains behind us, there was nothing but clear skies ahead. To the far north we could see the nearly 12,000 foot peak of Sierra Blanca in New Mexico and beneath us was the vast Chihuahuan desert that stretches for 795 miles from Arizona, New Mexico and West Texas, and far into Mexico. I pitied the Spanish explorers who crossed it on foot, not knowing if it would ever end. By the time they reached the Rio Grande River in the 1680s, they and their livestock were dying of thirst and heat exhaustion. It's a marvel any of them ever made it, and it is even more impressive that they and their many followers crossed it many times during the Spanish conquest.

Soon we could see in the distance an impressive peak jutting out of the desert floor. Guadalupe Peak, at 8,750 feet above sea level is the highest mountain in the state of Texas. From there on it was just flat desert as far as the eye could see. I had been enjoying the view and daydreaming when Gary said, "Looks like a little haze coming up." He looked at me as if to gauge my reaction.

I looked up ahead and saw a thin, wispy layer of clouds far below and said, "No problem. The weather report said it would be clear so this should blow over soon."

After a while, Gary said, "I can't see the highway anymore."

I looked down and saw that the cloud layer had gotten thicker and it stretched out before us in all directions. I quickly checked my map and our current compass heading. "Okay, then," I said. "Just keep it on this heading. When we get to where the airport should be, we'll start looking for a break in the cloud cover." To myself, I was cursing the darn weatherman who told me how clear it would be.

Nearly an hour later we had seen no break in the clouds and it became apparent that we were going to have to use our combined aviation skills to work out the problem. "Have you had any instrument training?" Gary asked, showing a little sign of concern.

"Uh, no," I answered. "Have you?"

"Heck no," he said. I haven't ever even been up this high. Our instructor taught us to fly like a crop duster—hugging the ground, and we only flew in good weather."

"Well, that's not going to help," I thought to myself. "Maybe I should take the controls," I said as I grasped the wheel. "I'm going to go down and start looking for a hole to get down through. Maybe if we zig-zag around a bit we can find a way down." It was becoming clear that we had already passed our destination and that if we could get under the cloud layer, we would have to double back and look for the airport. Worst case, I thought, we would just go back to El Paso and I would explain what happened. However, when I imagined the look on Mr. Zeiss's face, I became determined to find a way down.

At last, a good 20 minutes after passing the spot where the airport should have been, the thin cloud layer broke up and we were able to slide underneath. We doubled back and finally found the small airfield. We managed to land, deplane and take a short break. I made sure to sign the registry, proving I had actually been there. As we were boarding, Gary turned to me and asked, "Are you going to fill up?"

"No, that's not in the flight plan, besides I don't have enough money to fill up." I answered. "Do you have any money?"

"I just used it to buy a Coke," he replied.

"Well," I said, "Let's get going." We were soon airborne again, this time staying below the clouds until the sky cleared up. We were about to get back up to our assigned altitude when Gary said, "Hey, why don't we stay down low and chase some coyotes? That's what we used to do."

I would never have thought of that. It sounded like fun, so I said, "Okay, let's do it." I took the controls and dove the plane down to the desert floor and began flying along the nap of the earth, just above the sand dunes, the cactus and the creosote bushes. "Ride 'um cowboy," Gary yelled with excitement.

"Whoopie, let's go get 'um," I shouted ecstatically.

The rest of the trip back was spent scouring the countryside for coyotes, going hither and yon, and when we found one, we would circle back and scare the pants off him. Jack rabbits would scatter in all directions as we passed over. "This is what flying is all about," I thought. I had no idea flying could be this much fun. It was much better than flying way up high where you couldn't see the jack rabbits and all. But eventually, as we were approaching El Paso, I turned to Gary and said, "Well, the fun is over, I've gotta get you to Fabens fast and then go report in to Mr. Zeiss."

We landed at the Fabens airport and Gary got out. "That was great," he said. "Let's do it again."

"Okay," I said, but now my full attention was getting the plane back safely to El Paso. Soon, I was taxiing into the Southwest Air Rangers parking area and true to his word, Mr. Zeiss was on the tarmac waiting for me. I noticed right away that his arms were folded in front of him and he wore a deep scowl on his face. I barely had time get out of the plane when he was all over me.

"Where the hell have you been, Lewels?" he bellowed. "You're an hour and half late!"

Startled at his level of indignation, I stammered, "Well, we had headwinds."

"Both ways?" he yelled skeptically. "And who is 'we'?" he queried.

"Oh, just me and Betsy," I said thinking quickly. "That's what I call her," I said, patting the airplane's wing. I could tell he wasn't buying it.

"So you and Betsy had headwinds both ways? Is that your story?"

"Yessir," I answered assuredly. "She's a really good plane. I guess the winds shifted." At this point I knew I had to get out of there, so I turned and headed to the operations office to sign out. Zeiss was right behind me and right behind him was the maintenance man who was carrying a long dip stick.

I heard him say something to Mr. Zeiss and then Zeiss shouted out "One and half?" I turned back to see the maintenance man scowling at me and repeating, "Yes sir, only one and a half gallons of fuel left."

"Jesus Christ!" Zeiss yelled. "Where the hell did you go?"

"I went to the Midland-Odessa airport and signed in. You can check," I said. "You can call them and ask."

"I already did," he countered. "You were 45 minutes late getting there."

I just shrugged my shoulders as if there was nothing more to say, I turned away and headed for the door to the parking lot where my old 1953 Chevy was parked. I just wanted to get the heck out of there as fast as possible. As I was leaving the parking lot, I heard him yell. "You were running on fumes you idiot."

"What a grouch," I thought. After all, flying isn't an exact science. I wasn't going to let him ruin one of the best days of my life. "Ol' Betsy" and I had made the round trip without crashing and with no damage to the airplane. All's well that ends well. Besides, I had learned some important lessons that day. You just can't please everyone all of the time and you shouldn't take life so seriously. Every once in a while it's okay to just have fun, especially when you're facing the prospect of being sent halfway around the world to fight in a war you have no interest in fighting. Who knows if you'll ever make it back?

ROTC flight training. Left to right: Mr. Zeiss, Joe Lewels, John Anderson. In back is commandant of cadets at TWC, Col. Lavois. John Anderson also served in Vietnam as a Bird Dog pilot and survived.

Gary Miller (shown here in June, 1966) joined the U.S. Marine Corps upon graduation from Texas Western College (TWC). He was recruited by the Central Intelligence Agency upon completion of his military service and became a senior analyst specializing in top-secret satellite images. Upon his retirement, after 25 years of service, he was awarded the agency's highest honor, The Career Intelligence Medal. He said it was their second-highest medal, but "you have to die in the line of duty to get the top one. I told them I didn't want that one."

13

Chapter *Trece*

"Georgia Storm, the Girl from Boston"

Old Gringo was having the best time of his life in El Paso; he had even found a beautiful Mexicany girl to keep him company when we weren't working or getting into mischief. But neither of us could have dreamed how great our next adventure was about to be.

"I need to write a feature story for my journalism class by Monday, but I don't have any ideas," I told Gary as we were having lunch in the cafeteria of the Student Union Building, commonly known as the SUB. "Help me out here, give me some ideas."

Gary mulled over this request long and hard while he devoured his third taco. I could tell his mind was just not focused on my problem. He was probably thinking about that new girlfriend. Finally, he said, "Well why don't you write a story about your first solo cross country flight?" I could tell by the sly smile on his face that he was joking.

"No, I think I better let that one rest. I was lucky Mr. Zeiss didn't have me kicked out of the program. I'm pretty sure he figured out I wasn't 'solo' that day, but he can't prove a thing unless my 'solo' buddy rats on me," I said.

"So you don't think he bought the 'Ol Betsy' story?" he said laughingly.

"No, he definitely did not buy that story, but you have to admit that was pretty quick thinking on my part." I said proudly. "Besides, no harm done, right?"

"Yeah," Gary added, "except we almost ran out of gas and got ourselves killed! I told you we oughta have got some gas before coming back. We probably had enough to buy a couple of gallons at least."

"Okay, don't remind me," I said. "I guess all that fooling around, zig-zagging back and forth and back tracking used up more fuel than I thought. But I'm used to driving around on 'empty' all the time and I have never run out before."

"Yeah," Gary said, "'cept there's no gas stations up there you can just coast into."

"Well, that will never happen again! Lesson learned." I said philosophically.

Just then I noticed Gary's eyes focused on something across the room. I turned to see that a very attractive blonde had just entered the cafeteria, followed closely by a very dapper, elderly gentleman wearing an expensive suit. The girl didn't look like a student. She wore her hair piled up on top of her head and she was wearing a tight blouse and skirt with stockings and high heels.

"Wow! Who's that," Gary asked. "I've never seen her before."

"Rumor is that she is Georgia Storm, the stripper from the Waikiki Club in Juárez. They say the man is her agent," I explained.

Gary couldn't stop looking at her. Apparently there weren't many strippers attending his school in Big Lake. "Well, you're a reporter, why don't you just go over and interview her. That would be a great story."

"Gary, you're a genius!" I exclaimed. "That's what I'm going to do." But then a thought occurred to me. "There's a problem though. The rumor is that when she is asked if she is Georgia Storm she says she is."

"So what's the problem?" Gary asked.

"Well, what if she's lying. What if she isn't really a stripper?"

"Hmm," Gary was thinking over this problem. Finally, he said, "Well, hell, let's just go over to Juárez and interview the real one. That would solve the mystery."

"Gary," I said, "you're a lot smarter than you look. That idea just might work."

Gary looked very pleased with himself as he pushed his chair away from our table and stood up. "Where are you going?" I asked.

"I'm a fixin' to get me some more tacos. You want some?"

"No thanks, I'm a fixin' to go to the library," I answered mockingly. I would have paused to give him a brief grammar lesson, but my mind was already full of ideas for my new story. Besides, there would be plenty of time for that in the days ahead.

The next night, Gary and I drove across the bridge and parked my old 1953 Chevy on a back street near the Waikiki Club in downtown Ciudad Juárez. In those days, Juárez was kind of like Las Vegas minus the gambling. The main strip had huge neon signs advertising the many bars, stores, restaurants and strip clubs. The street was bustling with high school kids, college kids and soldiers from the army base, Fort Bliss. Pedestrians were immediately accosted by men peddling all manner of illicit activities. "Hey boys, you wanna go see the girls? You wanna go to Irma's?" was a common come on. "You wanna get married?" they would ask a couple. If they weren't looking to get married, he would ask, "You wanna divorce?" Juarez was famous as a place where you could get a quicky divorce and many famous American actors and actresses such as Frank Sinatra and Marilyn Monroe took advantage of that service. There were many illegal brothels hidden on back streets, the most famous being the previously mentioned "Irma's." But it was located away from the downtown area so taxi drivers were there offering young men a ride. They offered to take them there, wait for them (apparently a short wait) and bring them back safely. But on the main drag, the two largest strip joints were the "Follies" and "The Waikiki Club." These were sleazy enough, but many other, even sleazier ones existed on back streets such as "The Magic Cave" or "The White Lake." It took an experienced guide to find them and a sober one to keep everyone out of trouble. Because I spoke Spanish, I was often nominated to be the leader of the group.

Don't get me wrong; I was a willing guide, but my opinion of the backstreet joints was not a good one. It wasn't just that they were rundown and the girls weren't particularly attractive, it was that I was the only one who could understand what they were saying to each other about the boys. Their talk was all about who could get the most money out of them by getting them drunk on cheap booze. I was much more concerned about the diseases that one could get by doing something stupid. The "Pinocchio" in me always kicked in when I went to Juárez.

But tonight, Gary and I would only patronize the semi-classy Waikiki Club, just off the main drag. It was after 9:00 pm when we approached the glitzy, neon-covered signage which was bedecked with neon palm trees and hula girls. It was definitely a cheap version of a Las Vegas strip club, but for Gary it might as well have been Paris. "Gawlee," was all he could say as we sized up the words "Georgia Storm the Girl from Boston" on a huge sign above the door. Black and white glossy 8x10 photos of her wearing only a mink stole and striking different poses were displayed at the entrance where a hawker was shouting, "Come on in boys; take a look at the blonde beauty. Only $5 dollar cover charge and a two drink minimum. The show's gonna start soon. Come on in."

"Darn," Gary said, "I guess we'll each have to drink two drinks."

"Not me," I said. "I'm here on official business. You can have one of mine. I'm about to show you what a real investigative reporter can do."

We paid the cover charge and entered the dark cabaret, lighted mostly with black lights that made the white table cloths shine bright. The *maître di* showed us to a table next to the stage because we were almost an hour early for the 10:00 show, just to be sure we didn't miss the act. The stage had a small runway that passed next to our table and a four-piece band was playing in a back corner of the room. The emcee was just starting his spiel about the beautiful girls we were about to have the pleasure of viewing.

Just then the waiter came to take our drink orders. Since this was the big time, we didn't want to order some common drink like a Whiskey Sour or a Margarita, so I finally said, "I'll take two Congo Coolers," as if this were my ordinary preference. Gary, catching my drift said, "I'll have two Singapore Slings." We turned and grinned at each other. "Well, Gary, you finally made it to the big time. Just like Vegas." I joked.

Gary was too excited to catch the joke. The band was playing loudly and the emcee was trying to stir up the growing crowd of young men. "Okay boys, you wanna see the monkey? Come on, show me you want to see the monkey!" This weird off-color joke only managed to stir up a little, unenthusiastic applause. He seemed to give up with the jokes and went straight to the introductions. One at a time he would introduce the girls of the show. Each would come out and dance to the music, smile at the guys and try to engage some of the men in meaningless banter. Little by little each would take it off to more enthusiastic applause while a spotlight from the rear of the room followed them around the small stage. At the end of each performance the girl would take off her G string, prance around the stage one more time and dash behind the curtain.

Gary was applauding and eager for the star performer to be introduced. I, on the other hand, was furiously taking notes in my reporter's notepad. By the time Georgia came out, Gary had finished his Singapore Slings and I had passed one of my Congo Coolers over to him. I was nursing my only drink so as to have all my wits about me if I had the chance to interview the star after the show. I noticed every detail of the place and I even noticed Gary cleaning his glasses every few minutes. I decided to leave that detail out of my story.

Finally, the emcee announced the star attraction and left the stage for

Georgia to make her grand entrance. The band played the kind of stripper music you might have seen in the movies; the kind in which the drummer times his rhythm to the movements of the stripper, emphasizing each sharp movement of her hips from one side to the other, and then a little drum roll and another sharp "bang" as she rolls her hips and then gyrates her pelvis forward a number of times toward the audience. In strip-joint lingo, this is known as the "bumps and grinds." She was good at it and seemed to enjoy making a big show of it, as if she understood what a cliché it was.

Georgia was as attractive as her photos. Under the lighting she looked to be in her twenties and her blonde hair, blue eyes and white skin met with tumultuous applause by the now-full cabaret. She pranced around the stage in her mink stole making eye contact with those near the stage and smiling brightly as if she were having a great time. She danced for a while and then she flung her mink stole to the back of the stage and stood with her back to the audience stark naked. There would be no teasing the audience in her act. Then she turned around, she faced the audience with a big smile, wearing nothing but her high-heel shoes. The place went wild. She walked slowly to the end of the runway and stopped to allow the audience to scrutinize her supple and very well-shaped body. Gary and I were right there, staring straight up at her, uh legs. She looked down at us and laughed as if we were a couple of rubes, which we were.

Finally, she ended her act when someone from backstage threw out her mink stole and she put it on slowly while making one final round of the stage. Then she was gone.

I turned to Gary and asked, "Well what do you think?"

"She's great!" he answered.

"No, not that!" I scolded. "What do you think about whether or not she is the same girl we saw at the SUB."

"Oh, I forgot about that. I wasn't paying attention to that."

"Okay, then," I said, "I guess I'll just have to interview her."

"How are you gonna do that?" Gary asked, clearly not understanding the power of the press.

"Just watch," I said as I ripped a sheet of paper from my notepad and scribbled a message on it. I called the waiter over, slipped him a note and a dollar bill and asked him to deliver the note to Miss Storm. The note said: "Dear Miss Storm, we are reporters from the Texas Western College newspaper, *The Prospector*, and we would like to interview you. Would you please come to our table for a few minutes?"

The waiter disappeared with the note and we waited. "What did you write on the note?" Gary asked. After I told him, all he could say was "Genius, pure genius."

A few minutes later Georgia and one of the other strippers came out, fully clothed, and stood before us. "Hello boys." She said. I thought Gary might pass out. They didn't allow cameras in the place, but if I had one I wouldn't have bothered taking a picture of the girls, I would have loved getting a shot of Gary's face as he looked up adoringly at the girls. Priceless!

After we all introduced ourselves, Georgia and her friend "Misty" sat down and ordered a drink. I had to introduce Gary because at the moment he couldn't seem to get any words to come out of his mouth. As for Misty, that was the stage name for Georgia's friend who was another American girl in her twenties who had worked alongside Georgia for some time. She didn't want to be part of the story and she didn't give us her real name. "Miss Storm," I began, "there's a rumor going around campus that you're attending classes there, so we are here to find out if the rumor is true."

"You know," she began, "a lot of students have been in here asking me the same thing, so I'm happy to clear this up. No, I am not taking classes there. I wish I had time, but my schedule wouldn't allow me to do that."

"Well, that is that," I thought. I have my story. But the interview wasn't over and the girls weren't in any hurry to leave, so we had a nice long chat during which time I asked her for some details about who she was and how she landed in Juárez. I was also interested in knowing if she was really from Boston. The answer to that was "Yes, and proud of it."

Misty tried to get a few words in by asking Gary about himself, but he could hardly speak. "Your friend doesn't say much, does he?" she asked. "No, I said, he's kind of the silent type." I answered. But I knew that third drink had put him over the edge.

Finally, as the interview was about over, I asked for a publicity photo that I could turn in along with the story. "It would really help the story to have a picture of you," I suggested. At this, Georgia asked for my notebook and pen and she quickly jotted down her home address and phone number in El Paso. "This is top secret information," she warned. "You can't share this with anyone."

"No, no, I wouldn't do that," I assured her.

"Ok, then, come by tomorrow around noon, but call first. I'll have the photo for you there." With that, she and Misty said goodbye, turned and disappeared backstage. Gary and I were left standing, he with his goofy look on his face and me with the top-secret note in my hand. I called the waiter over and whispered into his ear: "*La cuenta es para mi amigo,*" then I excused myself and went to the men's room.

On the way back over the bridge, Gary just kept saying, "That was great, that was really great." His greatest expectations of what college life should be had just been exceeded beyond his wildest dreams. As for me, I was now certain that I had made the right choice in choosing journalism as a college major. I felt I had a certain knack for it. If I could interview a stripper and get a great story, I could interview anyone. Gary, on the other hand had chosen to be a psychology major, a choice that at the moment seemed a bit lackluster.

"So," I asked, "you want to come with me tomorrow to pick up the photo?"

"Absolutely!" he exclaimed. "Besides, you may need a bodyguard."

"Okay, then, I'll pick you up just before noon."

I went home, went straight to my typewriter and hammered out the rough draft of the story. I would proofread and rewrite the story on Sunday

THE PROSPECTOR

1913-1963: TWC's Golden Jubilee

VOL. XXX — EL PASO, TEXAS, MARCH 14, 1964

Too Bad, Boys
Stripper Bares Non-TW Status

By JOE LEWELS

Texas Western students have been known to have strange hobbies, but combining the grind of school work with the bumps and grinds of the stripping profession would be a new one, even for a border city.

The SUB buzzes like a disturbed beehive every time a certain blonde is seen traipsing through the lunch line.

"Hey, look at that! Isn't that Georgia Storm?"

"Sure, didn't you know? She's a student here in the day and a stripper in Juarez at night."

The rumors have Miss Storm supporting a family and going to college, so she can quit the "racket."

NOT A STUDENT

Georgia, who is Rosemary DeVarti off-stage, does not attend TWC, has no family and hasn't the slightest intention of quitting the "racket." As a matter of fact, she is quite proud of her profession and is flattered that anyone would mistake her for a college student.

Georgia is a short, well-shaped blonde with a charming personality and a self-confident smile that comes from a lifetime of performing.

"College students have been coming in here often asking me if I really go to school. Some say that I'm in their classes and some even accuse me of being an imposter, saying that the real Georgia Storm doesn't strip anymore because she is going to Texas Western," she said.

SHE'S FLATTERED

Miss Storm added as an afterthought, "You know, I'm beginning to feel that anytime now someone's going to say, 'Will the real Georgia Storm please stand up?'? I wish they would, so I could clear this matter up. It really is annoying at times, yet I am flattered because the kids

Stripteaser Not A Coed

(Continued from Page 1)

ally Houston, where she began her stripping career.

She obviously enjoys her work and takes great pride in it. From a small stage, amidst a roar of catcalls and whistles, clouds of smoke, flashing spotlights and dim ultra-violet lights, she performs her dance, shedding her garments to the delight of the crowd who try to see everything they can, but who usually end up thinking they saw much more than they did.

"I don't think my work is anything to be ashamed of; it's a profession just like acting or singing, and not any girl can perform without being booed off the stage," Miss Storm said.

WOULD LIKE SCHOOL

"I would like very much to take some courses at the College, but working late at night doesn't leave much time for going to school," she said.

On an average day, Miss Storm, who lives in El Paso, does her grocery shopping, visits her hairdresser or her banker, and keeps busy with rehearsals in the late afternoons.

Bowling, tennis, badminton and bicycle riding are her favorite hobbies, and according to "Misty," a beautiful blonde from Dallas, who co-stars in the show, "Georgia is a great cook."

The delightful Miss Storm adds this comment with a slight wink, "Any college girls who would like to have a new hobby are welcome to come to the show and get a first-hand demonstration of how the experts do it."

"Georgia Storm the Girl from Boston."

and turn it in along with the photo on Monday, just making my deadline.

The next day, Saturday, I phoned Georgia, picked Gary up and we drove to the address she had given me. Gary didn't look good. In fact, he had a terrible hangover. "What the hell do they put in those Singapore Slings?" he asked. He could barely open his eyes.

I just shrugged my shoulders. "Hell if I know." I said.

Georgia lived in an apartment house close to the downtown area of El Paso. We parked and went up to the second floor and knocked on the door. We were a little nervous. Neither of us had ever been to the apartment of a stripper. So, we were surprised when it was Misty who opened the door. "Hi boys," she said casually. "Come on in and have a seat." She looked a little older in the light of day. She wasn't wearing makeup and she had her hair pulled back in a ponytail. Gary and I sat down on the couch in the small living room and shortly Georgia came out from the bedroom carrying a manila envelope. She and misty were both wearing jeans and blouses and I noticed they were both barefoot. She handed me the envelope and I opened it and pulled out the photo. It was identical to the one in the display case at the Waikiki Club. It showed Georgia wearing her mink stole and nothing else. Gary and I noticed the great amount of cleavage that was showing. I was thinking that the newspaper's faculty sponsor might not like that very much, but what could I do?

In the cold light of day, the girls looked older and not so sexy. They were both pushing 30 I thought, but the cabaret lights made them appear much younger—so did the drinks. It seemed clear that the two lived together in the small one-bedroom apartment and years later we would ponder the idea that they might have been a couple. However, at the moment, we were both way too unworldly to have noticed such a thing or even consider the possibility. They asked if we would like a cup of coffee, but we declined and we left the apartment a little let down. "They just weren't that sexy in the daylight. They just seemed like regular people," Gary remarked. Even so, we were both a little giddy on the ride home, after all how many students had been to a famous stripper's apartment? None! Gary had something to write home about and I knew I had a great story. I was revved up to finalize the draft and get it submitted to the newspaper.

On Monday morning I hand carried the article and the photo to the newsroom, but was told that the faculty sponsor who was also my professor (Ralph Lowenstein) was in the faculty lounge. The editor told me I would have to hurry to get the story in the upcoming weekly edition of the paper, so I barged into the faculty lounge and found him sitting with some of the other professors. He was somewhat disturbed that a student would bother him in the lounge that was off-limits to students. "I am so sorry to bother you here," I said, "but the deadline for the newspaper is in two hours and the editor said you would have to approve my feature story before they could run it." I could see he was annoyed, but his expression changed quickly when he pulled the story and the photo out of the envelope. His eyes widened and he raised his eyebrows when he saw Georgia in her mink stole. He quickly read the story and his eyes got even wider. Then he stood up and pulled me aside to get some privacy. He obviously didn't want anyone to see the photo. "This is a good story, Lewels. But we can't run the picture unless we do some airbrushing. There's just too much cleavage showing. Take it back to the editor and tell her I approve the story, but they'll have to airbrush the picture. Hurry up."

That week's edition of *The Prospector* was the fastest sellout ever. Not that students had to pay for it, because it was free. Stacks of papers would be placed in bins all over campus and anyone could pick up a copy at will. Nevertheless, there were always plenty of copies left over by the next week's edition. Not this time. The front page story with the large photo of Georgia in her mink stole had a headline that read: "Stripper Bares Non-TW Status." The lead paragraph, always the most important one in a good news story, read: "Texas Western students have been known to have strange hobbies, but combining the grind of school work with the bumps and grinds of the stripping profession would be a new one, even for a border city." The byline read: "by Joe Lewels."

The story ran in the March 14, 1964 issue of the newspaper and later that year it won first place in the Texas Intercollegiate Press Association awards competition for "best news feature story." What can I say? Thanks in great part to my friend Gary, I was famous again.

You may be wondering who that student was who created such a hubbub in the SUB that day. The simple answer is that I don't know. She and her Mexicany escort were never seen again after the story came out. No one seemed to know her name or where she went. The rumor mill, however, was buzzing with new information. In one version of the story, she was a student from Jal, a small community in Southeastern New Mexico, and the older man was her "sugar daddy," or in other words, she was his mistress. It was said that he was a dentist from Juárez. But these are just rumors. If she had been seen again, I would have liked to interview her for a follow-up story. Maybe that was exactly what she was worried about. That part of the story will always remain a mystery.

The week after the story came out, Gary and I were having lunch at Fred's Rainbow Bar in Juárez, enjoying a cold Cruz Blanca beer and reminiscing about our latest adventure. "Well," I said, "I guess Big Lake will never look quite the same after life on the border."

"You're right. No one back home would believe me if I told them about meeting Georgia Storm, and I can't very well send my folks a copy of the story. They might make me come back home," Gary replied. "I guess with the marines and the war I probably won't be going back to live there, maybe ever."

"I still wish you would enroll in ROTC and go into the army with me. Maybe we could serve in the same unit." I suggested.

"Naw, the army's for sissies," Gary teased. "The marines is where the action is."

"That's just the problem," I replied. "The idea is to stay away from the action."

But Gary's mind was made up; after we graduated in 1966, he joined the marines and was sent to Quantico, VA. for basic training. I, on the other hand, was waiting to receive my orders to enter the U.S. Army as a brand-new second lieutenant. The war in Vietnam was not going to end in time for either of us to miss it; in fact it was escalating. Our days of fun were over and life was about to get serious real soon.

Sadly, I wouldn't get to see Gary for several years, but we kept in touch, first by regular mail and eventually by email where he adopted the screen name of "Old Gringo." I guess his years on the border made an indelible impression on him. Amazingly, Gary missed the war due to a knee injury he sustained during basic training. The marines then assigned him to their photo analysis department where he learned to analyze aerial pictures taken by U.S. spy planes in Vietnam. This skill was what ultimately brought him to the attention of the CIA. He sent me a post card after his knee injury. It said: "I'm a fixin' to be a photo analyst and as soon as my knee heals up, I'm going to try out for the 'rasslin team."

Many years passed but Gary and I never lost touch. He spent the following 25 years after his service in the marines getting married, having two beautiful daughters and working as an image analyst at the CIA. Because I was the only person who knew that he worked there and because he trusted me, he told me a little about what his work was like. Upon his retirement, he wrote to me and said, "My job at the agency was imagery analysis. I was charged with analyzing satellite images revealing information about military aircraft, like the Mig-29, as well as air-launched missile systems. As a senior analyst at the agency, my conclusions were often sought after throughout the intelligence community. For some reason, my analysis was very predictive. I could predict future outcomes of projects I saw on the photos with great accuracy, even though the outcomes were several years into the future. Some people thought I was psychic. Upon retirement, the agency presented me with the Career Intelligence Medal, which is the second highest medal they give out. You have to die in the line of duty to get the top one. I told them I didn't want that one."

As we grew older, our conversations became more serious. In one of his letters he told me of a bizarre experience he had when he was involved in a serious automobile accident while at the agency. He was so badly injured that he was taken to the trauma unit of a nearby hospital and while there, he felt the life leaving his body.

"The next thing I knew I was floating up to the ceiling in one corner of the room. I hovered there watching the doctors and nurses working on my carcass. For a while, I actually felt it was amusing that they were sweating so hard over a lifeless body. I was completely relaxed, unafraid and at peace. A very bright light was shining through the wall behind me. I knew I could go to it if I wanted to. It was as if it was giving me a choice. Then suddenly, I decided to reoccupy my body and I swooped down and reentered through the right side of my head…Ever since then I have known that I will be okay- when I die. You are the first person I've told of this experience. I wish we were sitting at Fred's Rainbow Bar having a sandwich and a cool one discussing this stuff. Maybe someday. Old Gringo."

A few months after his retirement our communications stopped. One day, his wife called me and said, "Gary died of a massive heart attack. I know he would want you to know."

After offering my sincere condolences and having a brief conversation, I hung up the phone. Then, to my surprise, I cried as if I had lost a brother. I took his death hard. I had never imagined that we might never see each other again. I was sure there were many more adventures in store for us someday. Gary's was that special kind of friendship that lasts a lifetime and for that I am forever grateful. God bless you Old Gringo; I'm sure we will meet again. Maybe we can even convince God to arrange for us to have one last Cruz Blanca beer together, but probably not at a strip club.

14

Chapter *Catorce*
One Taco Short

On the border we sometimes refer to a person who isn't too bright as being "one taco short of a combination plate." That was a good description of me when I was 12. At that advanced age, I was still not smart enough to know what adults did when the kids weren't looking. Remember, this was at a time when television and movies always showed parents sleeping in separate beds and wearing pajamas. It was forbidden by law for actors to say the word "pregnant" on TV. Love scenes consisted of an adult man kissing an adult woman on a date, while fully clothed. The picture would fade to black and in the next scene they were blissfully taking their new baby home from the hospital.

America, it seemed, wanted its kids to grow up as dumb as possible, and I was its prime example. In my imagination, the dirtiest thing I could think up that adults might be doing to make babies was that they would get naked and rub their butts together. I even took this a step further and imagined that when they got together with other adults at parties, everyone would get naked and rub butts with everyone else. I could see how this might be fun for them. But still, it was hard to see how this activity could result in the making of a baby. It was a mystery. My ignorance was due to the fact that

MY PARENTS NEVER TOLD ME ANYTHING! It took me many more years to figure things out on my own by doing something I rarely did—I went to the public library and looked it up.

I am sure you think by now I am ready to give you the details of my findings, but alas, this chapter isn't about sex; it's about how I had to get smart slowly by uncovering all the secrets my parents and my schools conspired to keep away from me. It seems that around every corner there were more secrets for me to unravel. It was as if I was living in a murder mystery and I had to find the clues that were cleverly hidden in plain sight.

One day, as a freshman in college, for some reason, I needed my birth certificate, so I asked my mom, "Hey mom, do you have a copy of my birth certificate?" I thought this was a simple request. However, the expression on her face told me immediately that there was a problem.

"Why do you need it?" she asked with a bit of consternation. She would have made a terrible poker player as every thought that passed through her head instantly registered on her face.

"I just do," I answered a bit peeved. "Why does it matter? Do you have it or don't you?"

"Well I'll look for it; I'm not sure where it is." I could tell she was stalling. "Give me a few days."

"No mom, I need it now!" I pressed. "I'll help you look if you want me to."

A worried look crossed her face and then, reluctantly, she retreated into her bedroom and started looking through drawers full of papers, old receipts, Christmas cards and junk.

It took her several minutes fumbling with boxes of papers before she emerged with an old, yellowing envelope. She carefully pulled out my birth certificate and handed it to me with that worried look on her face. I unfolded the delicate document carefully and began to examine it as if I were a police detective looking for a clue. The date of birth, April 10, 1944, was correct; it had me listed as a Caucasian, not a Mexican, which was good; the city was

El Paso and name of the doctor seemed legit. It all seemed to be in order. My parents were really my parents, or so it appeared. So what was she worried about? But then I noticed the name of the hospital at the top of the document. It said: "Newark Maternity Clinic."

"Mom," I asked, "what is the Newark Maternity Clinic? I thought I was born at Southwestern General Hospital? You always told me I was born at Southwestern General."

Her eyes widened and her mouth scrunched up. She had been caught in a lie. But why? "Well," she said, "I didn't want you to know."

"Know what?" I exclaimed. "I don't get it. Where is the Newark Maternity Clinic anyway?" I asked.

Her face bore the expression of a kid who had been caught with her hand in the cookie jar.

"Well, when you were born things weren't going very well with us because of the war and we couldn't afford Southwestern General. So we went to the free clinic in South El Paso. I wanted you to believe you had been born in a better place. I was ashamed."

"Well that's just the silliest thing I've ever heard of. Why would I care where I was born? The only thing that matters is that I was born and that I am still alive today. I don't care where I was born! You didn't have to keep that a secret," I chastised. But now I started to get a little paranoid. There were just too many secrets in my family! You can't blame me for being a bit suspicious. "Maybe the document was a forgery. Maybe I was adopted. Maybe I was stolen as a baby from my real parents who were rich New Yorkers who just happened to be passing through town," I thought. So I just came out and asked.

"Is this certificate real?"

"Yes, of course it's real." She said confidently.

"I wasn't adopted?" I asked.

"No, of course not," she answered.

"Are you and Dad hiding anything else from me?" I said, raising my voice. "Like maybe you're both Russian spies?" I asked in jest.

"No, no," she said laughingly. "Don't be silly. Not me. Ask your father about that."

"Ask him about what? Are you saying he's a spy?" I asked in amazement.

"No, no, he just thinks he's in the CIA. But he's crazy."

"So let me get this straight. You're saying that Dad thinks he is in the CIA?" I asked incredulously.

"You'll just have to ask him about that," she answered, disarmingly.

"Mom, you don't really think dad is in the CIA, do you?" I pleaded.

"Talk to him about that. Yes, he thinks he's in the CIA, but he's nuts. You'll have to ask him," she said, ending the conversation.

That evening after dinner I sat my dad down in the living room and came right to the point. "Dad, are you in the CIA?"

"No, of course not. Where did you ever get that idea?" he answered.

"Well, Mom seems to think that you believe you're in the CIA." I said.

"Oh, she exaggerates everything. I'm not in the CIA, I just talk to them every once in a while."

"You talk to the CIA every once in a while?" I asked with great skepticism.

"Oh God," I thought, "Maybe both my parents are really crazy. Maybe that is the real secret."

"Yes, they come to see me every once in a while or I meet them in Mexico City," he continued. "But you can't tell anyone. It's top secret."

Now my head was reeling. I still didn't believe this story could be true. "Why didn't you tell me?" I asked.

"Because it's a secret," he said, assuredly.

"Okay," I said, trying to remain calm. "Then what do they talk to you about?"

"Well, it's a long story, but it started when I was covering the Mexican elections many years ago for the newspaper and the wire services. You know about that don't you?" he asked.

"Sure, I know about that."

"Well, during those days, I became very friendly with the candidate who was running for president of Mexico for the PAN party against the PRI party.

The PRI party is very leftist. They have ruled Mexico through corruption for more than 40 years and they support Fidel Castro. Castro and his revolutionaries lived in Mexico City while they were planning the takeover in Cuba. Russia supports Castro and they are trying to get communist infiltrators into key political positions in Mexico. It's a mess. Our government is very worried that communism will spread throughout Latin America."

"Okay," I said, "but where does the CIA come in?"

"Well," he explained, "I have very good sources in Mexico, which I have cultivated over many years. We keep in touch and the U.S. government is very interested in what I find out. So, a long time ago I was contacted by the CIA and they asked if I would share information with them and I told them I would."

"So you do work for the CIA," I asked, seeking clarification.

"Well, they don't pay me. We just exchange information. I tell them what I know and they tell me what's going on in the State Department and what's going on behind the scenes. I use their information in the stories I write for the wire services as a stringer, but some of it I can't write about."

"What kind of information?" I asked.

"For example, I knew about last year's Bay of Pigs invasion of Cuba well before it happened. But it was top secret."

"I don't understand why they would share that kind of information with you if you don't work for them."

"They trust me because they know I am as much against Castro and communism as they are, and they've known me for a long time," he explained.

"I thought the Bay of Pigs invasion was just about a bunch of crazy Cuban exiles," I said.

"Yes, but they were trained and armed by the CIA in secret bases here in the U.S. Also, the CIA has been trying to kill Castro with the help of the Mafia," he continued. "But you can't tell anyone. That's still top secret."

"That's crazy, Dad," I complained. "Why would the CIA be dealing with the Mafia? That doesn't make sense."

"The Mafia hates Castro as much as the CIA because Castro threw them out of Cuba and confiscated their gambling casinos. And the Mafia knows how to assassinate people in a way that keeps the U.S. out of it."

"I can't believe President Kennedy would allow that!" I said emphatically.

"I'm not so sure he can control everything the CIA does." He explained. "He certainly didn't support the Bay of Pigs invasion, because when it failed, he refused to send in air support to help the exiles. They were slaughtered on the beaches and many were taken prisoners. Now the Cuban-Americans hate Kennedy and so does the CIA and the Mafia."

"The Mafia?" I asked. "Why does the Mafia hate him?"

"They don't like the fact that Kennedy's brother, Bobby, who is attorney general, is getting real tough, trying to put them all behind bars and breaking up their organization," he explained.

"But that's a good thing, isn't it?" I asked.

"Sure, but it's complicated," he answered.

"I don't know, Dad, that all seems very farfetched. Are you sure about all this?"

"Yes, I'm sure," he answered definitively.

"So what proof do you have that any of what you're saying is true?"

"Well, I can't prove it, but I have plenty of evidence that the U.S. State Department has been following my stories. Here, I'll show you." With that, he went into his bedroom/office and came out with several files of papers. "Look at these letters from the Secretary of State's office, and here's an issue of the Congressional Record that has some of my stories printed verbatim. That's the official record of what happens in Congress."

I looked over the evidence and there was no doubt. My dad, whose business often took him to Mexico, had definitely been in contact with the State Department and members of Congress. He certainly had plenty of opportunities to meet with anti-communist leaders and with agents of the Central Intelligence Agency. Besides, I had no reason to doubt him. I had to conclude that my dad was not nuts and that he was, in fact, an unpaid informer for the CIA. I was shocked. "I can't believe I didn't know all this. It's been going on for years. How come you didn't tell me?" I asked.

"This is top secret information. You're old enough to know and understand now, but you were too young before. I know you can keep a secret. You can't tell anyone about this, okay?"

"Yes, sure," I said. "I promise."

Back then, my dad seemed quite self-assured about his strong anti-communist leanings, but the day would come when his zealousness was tested in a very personal way. Several years later, in 1966, as I prepared to leave to serve a tour in Vietnam, I approached him with a minor request. "Dad, I need you to hold on to this for me while I'm gone," I said as I thrust a white envelope toward him. "What is it," he asked wearily. "It's my last will and testament," I stated. "You're the executor."

His reaction was visceral. "No, no, I don't want it he shouted as he pushed it away and turned his head so I wouldn't see the tears in his eyes. "Don't give it to me!"

"But Dad, it's just routine. We are all required to have one. I'll just leave it on your desk."

He turned back to me, tears streaming down his cheeks, his face twisted with pain as he pleaded, "I don't want you to go. Please don't go. You can go to Mexico and live with your cousins."

"But Dad, I'm going to fight against communism. Don't you want that?" That declaration stopped him cold. He paused for a long time thinking over what I had said. It was as if he had never considered how the war on communism could affect his family directly. Finally, he said, "I don't care about that. All I care about is you. Please don't go," he cried.

"I've got to go, dad. I don't want to be a fugitive from the law the rest of my life. I thought you were proud of me for becoming an officer and doing my duty."

"Yes, of course I am proud of you, but that doesn't matter now. I just don't want to lose you," he said, completely breaking down in sobs. It was the first time I ever saw him cry and the first time I realized just how much he loved me. I hugged him and said, "I love you Dad. Don't worry, I'll be back." Then I left to do my duty, even though I had no desire to serve in the military and I hadn't an inkling of why we were waging a war in a far off little country on the other side of the world. I had no choice. But that took place in 1966 after I graduated from college. My dad first confided in me about his CIA connections in 1962.

By the beginning of my sophomore year at TWC, in 1963, I had become my dad's closest confidant when it came to his secret liaisons with the CIA. One day he pulled me aside to tell me about his latest covert meeting. "I saw them again yesterday," he said secretively. "We met downtown at the Hotel Paso Del Norte, in the lobby. They were very happy. They said it would be over soon. Something big was going to happen that would change everything."

"What is it?" I asked excitedly.

"I think they're finally going to get rid of Castro," he said in whispered tones, as if the room were bugged. "That's what I think."

"So they didn't say exactly what was going to happen?"

"No. It must be very hush hush," he said.

The date of our conversation was mid to late November of 1963. We were both on high alert for notice that Castro was dead.

I was in English class when it happened. After the bell rang and the students filed out into the halls in the Liberal Arts Building, a friend of mine rushed up to me and said. "Have you heard?"

"Heard what," I asked.

"President Kennedy has been shot. It happened in Dallas."

The words hit me like blast from a gun. I had to take a step backward. I couldn't believe it. Could this be what the CIA agents were referring to? Was Kennedy the real target all along? I rushed home to watch the news on TV like everyone else in the country. Walter Cronkite, the renowned news anchorman for CBS news, was almost in tears as he announced that it was official. President Kennedy was dead. I cried along with so many other Americans. How could this have happened in America? I wondered. But in the back of my mind I thought I knew.

Then my dad walked in. He was white as a sheet and obviously scared. I looked at him and he looked at me. We both knew what the other was thinking. We knew that neither of us could ever talk about this again. All we could do is watch the terrible event unfold. But when the Warren Commission announced its finding that a lone gunman, Lee Harvey Oswald, was solely responsible, Dad and I were pretty sure there was much more to the story, but we had no proof.

The CIA men never called or met with my dad again as far as I know.

In his book, *With Kennedy*, Pierre Salinger, JFK's press secretary, wrote in 1965 that the Bay of Pigs invasion had been planned under the Eisenhower/Nixon administration by the CIA and the top generals at the Pentagon. In October of 1960, three months before Kennedy took office, the story of the impending invasion had been leaked and the media began reporting that the U.S. was training a brigade for military action against Castro. Any hope of a surprise attack had been dashed.

Because Kennedy had beaten Richard Nixon in the November 1960 election, the ill-conceived and poorly-planned fiasco fell into Kennedy's lap as he entered office in January 1961, putting him in an impossible situation. He would bear responsibility in the eyes of the public for the outcome, but he was pressured to follow the advice of the CIA and the top military leaders. Castro was waiting for them with Russian, airplanes, tanks and other armaments and the invasion was crushed in just three days.

Sending in U.S. troops to aid the Cuban exiles had never been part of the plan for fear of starting a war with Russia, yet JFK was blamed for not doing so. Kennedy's response as quoted by Salinger was: "How could the crowd at the CIA and the Pentagon be this wrong?" It was a hard lesson for the new president, who would somehow have to gain control of the over-zealous generals and CIA cloak-and-dagger men who had conspired in the ill-fated mission, which led to the Soviets sending nuclear missiles to Cuba. This, of course, triggered the infamous Cuban-Missile Crisis the following year.

In the end, the person blamed for the Kennedy assassination, Lee Harvey Oswald, it turned out, was deeply involved in the Cuban controversy. A former marine who defected to the Soviet Union and married a Russian, he returned to the U.S. and joined the "Fair Play for Cuba Committee," a pro-communist and pro-Castro group who vehemently opposed the invasion of Cuba. His connection to the Cuban controversy was undeniable. This led Salinger to write: "Only in the U.S. is the report of the Warren Commission, fixing the sole responsibility on Oswald, widely believed."

Who wanted Kennedy dead?

A lot of people. But in my mind the assassination was not the act of a lone gunman. I still believe Oswald was the patsy who would take the fall but there were others involved. Years laters, when I was working in Washington for the Department of Justice (DOJ) in 1972, the headquarters of the Democratic National Committee was burglarized—the infamous Watergrate break in. Since the DOJ director at the time, Richard Kleindienst, was one of the few conspirators who actually served jail time, I naturally followed the case very closely. It turned out to be Cuban exiles and ex-CIA and FBI men workng under the direction of our Republican president, Richard Nixon, who were guility. I thought that very curious and it reminded me of what happened to JFK.

(Author's note: In October of 2017 a trove of almost 3000 formerly classified documents regarding the Kennedy assassination were released to the public. They confirmed my father's story that the CIA and the mafia had been trying to kill Fidel Castro. The documents also revealed that persons of interest in the killing of Kennedy included mafia bosses Santo Trafficante and Meyer Lansky. Also under suspicion were future Watergate burglars Bernard Baker, Frank Sturgis and a number of Cuban exiles. All of these were involved in the Bay of Pigs invasion and were CIA operatives. All were Kennedy haters.)

15

Chapter *Quince*

Getting Smart the Hard Way

The first thing you learn in the army is that there are three ways to do anything: the right way, the wrong way and the army way. I found out there was one more: the hard way.

By June 1966, Gary Miller and I had managed to graduate college, Gary headed to the marines and I was waiting for my orders to see where the army would be sending me. I was about to begin serving two years of active duty as a second lieutenant (the lowest officer rank), but in which branch? That was the question. The army held my future in its hands and the wait was excruciating.

The day the orders arrived, direct from the Pentagon, all the graduating ROTC cadets were gathered outside the office of the commandant of cadets, Colonel Lavois, nervously waiting for their names to be called. As I mentioned previously, the army had generously given us all a choice in the matter by having us complete a form earlier in the year asking us to list the three branches of the army which we felt best suited us. I had filled in the blanks as follows: 1. Intelligence Corps 2. Signal Corps. 3. Transportation Corps.

My reasoning for my choices were quite logical, I believed. As a journalism major, I had been well trained in the gathering of intelligence (news), analyzing all the facts and putting all the pieces of the puzzle together in the form of a report (news story). As proof of my abilities to serve as an intelligence agent, I pointed out the investigation I had conducted on the mystery of the beautiful blonde: Georgia Storm, the girl from Boston. As a journalist, I was trained, not only to dig up facts, but to see the larger picture, as only one who is trained in the liberal arts can do. I felt I was the perfect choice for the Army Intelligence Corps.

Besides, how intelligent do you have to be to be assigned to Army Intelligence? It's not as if the words "army" and "intelligence" go together anyway. The word "oxymoron" comes to mind immediately. I was quite certain that the army brass would easily conclude that I was a natural choice for that branch. They needed me on so many levels that it was hard for me to consider any other outcome.

As for my next two choices, I just threw them in because the form required the applicant to list three choices. The Signal Corps seemed logical because those folks are all about communication, and that was what I was trained for. If for some reason, the army made a mistake, or all the Intelligence positions had been filled, I could be quite happy in the Signal Corps. In fact, I felt supremely overqualified for this branch of the army and I was certain the generals in the Pentagon would surely agree with this point.

The Transportation Corps was simply an afterthought. Anyone with a driver's license should qualify for that one. I only wrote that one down to make it clear to the people at the Pentagon that I had no real interest in, talents for, or discernible qualifications for being assigned to the infantry or any other branch that would ever get me involved in any real fighting or in a position in which I would be required to slog through rice paddies, waiting to be ambushed. Or where I might get dirty.

As for becoming an army aviator, that was not really part of the plan.

There was no branch for army aviation. A pilot could serve in any branch of the army and still be an aviator. Furthermore, aviation school was strictly voluntary, in spite of the fact the army paid for my private pilot's license. At this point, I could see no reason to serve an extra year of active duty just to go to flight school. No, I felt the Intelligence Corps was the right place for me and for the army. It was a win-win situation all around.

Finally, my name was called. "Lewels," shouted out the colonel's secretary, holding up a brown, manila envelope. I took it and anxiously broke it open. Inside were two sheets of army jibberish, which I couldn't understand, but a few words stood out clearly: "Fort Belvoir, Virginia," and "Corps of Engineers." I had to sit down before I could read it again after taking a few deep breaths to help me calm down. On the second reading, the message seemed clear. These orders were meant for someone who had asked to go into the Corps of Engineers, therefore they could not be mine. There had to be another person named Francisco Jose. That was it. It was a simple mistake.

I took the two sheets of paper over to the secretary and said, "There's been a big mistake. These aren't my orders."

She took them from me and perused them, then she asked, "Is your name Francisco Jose Lewels?"

"Yes ma'am," I said.

"Well then, they're yours," she said handing them back to me.

"But I didn't ask for the engineers, I'm a journalism major." I explained in desperation. "The army has made a big mistake."

"No lieutenant," she said. "The army doesn't make mistakes."

I couldn't tell if she really believed what she just said or if she was just toying with me. From the look on her face I could tell she meant it.

"Well, they did this time!" I argued vehemently.

"Look, lieutenant, there's nothing I can do. You want to see the colonel?"

"Yes, yes I do."

"Well go on in, he's in his office," she said pointing to the door behind her.

I went into the colonel's office and didn't waste time. "Colonel, there's been a big mistake. My orders say Corps of Engineers, but I'm a journalism major. I didn't ask for the engineers! You need to call the Pentagon and get this fixed."

"Let me take a look at those orders," he said as if this was no big deal. He took them and read them with some care before he looked back up at me. "Well, you are "Francisco Jose Lewels" aren't you?" he asked.

"Yes sir." I said. "But I don't belong in the engineers. I barely got through algebra."

The colonel spent a few pensive moments considering what this could all mean and what his options were, then he said, "These orders look right to me. You know, the army needs engineers right now," as if that was a rational explanation.

"That may be, but I am not one." I argued. "I don't know anything about being an engineer. I have trouble changing a flat tire on my car," I said in my defense. "Please, you need to get on the phone to the Pentagon and tell them they made a mistake. I want to transfer to another branch."

"There's nothing I can do. Orders are orders," he said. "But don't worry," he said in a calming voice, "they'll train you at Fort Belvoir. They'll turn you into an engineer in no time."

"But these orders say the course is only eight weeks long; that's not enough time to turn me into an engineer!"

At that, he pushed the orders back to me across the desk and threw up his hands. "Sorry lieutenant, there's nothing I can do. You can write your congressman if you want to, but that probably won't do any good either."

Well, that was it. I turned, head held low and started to walk out of his office when he said, "Try to look at the bright side, they could have put you in the infantry."

That thought had not yet crossed my mind, but at that moment I knew the colonel was right. There was a silver lining to this dark cloud—I wasn't going into the infantry. At least that.

On that very long drive from El Paso to Virginia I had plenty of time to ponder all the possibilities that could have torpedoed my plan to be assigned to the Army Intelligence Corps, or at least to one of my other choices. At first I thought the army simply never intended to accede to my wishes in the first place. The whole thing was just a ruse. Having new lieutenants complete that form must be a psychological ploy to make us think we actually have choices, when in fact we didn't. The form was devised by the Pentagon psychological warfare department as a means of getting us accustomed to the notion that the army was now fully in charge of our lives. Questioning their authority would be futile. Yes, I thought, that could be it. Futility was the lesson! Diabolical is what it was. The form was the beginning of a long, slow process of brainwashing officers. The process was essential for the army's goal of turning us into docile, robotic fighting machines. Struggling against the institution would never work. We would have to learn to follow any order we were given blindly. We had to learn how to obey without questioning any order we received. "Very clever," I thought, "very clever indeed."

But after driving a few more hundred miles and still not having left the state of Texas, I began to doubt my theory. I began to see there was one big hole in that diabolical plan. That hole, I could now begin to see, was that the army just isn't that clever. As a whole, the army is a huge, bumbling, by-the-book, bureaucracy hardly clever enough to hatch such a complicated scam. No, I could now see that the most likely scenario was that some clerk somewhere just lost the form. I could imagine a young corporal sitting at a desk at the Pentagon with a huge stack of forms in his "in box" and a steaming cup of coffee in his hand. "Oops," he said as he spilled the coffee on the forms, ruining them. "Oh well," he said as he brushed them into his trash can. "They were a month overdue anyway." Who would care? He probably just got some blank forms and started assigning new lieutenants randomly to the branches of the army.

"Yes, that's what happened," I thought. It was just a typical army screw up. The forms just weren't that important to begin with.

But, by the time I was driving through Tennessee, I was beginning to think that it might have been that my past finally caught up with me. I envisioned a meeting of Army brass that reviewed each new lieutenant's thick dossier to determine where each should be placed. "Oh this is rich," one of them might have said. "This guy wants to be assigned to the Intelligence Corps, but look at these transcripts and report cards. He wasn't the brightest bulb in the first grade."

"And it didn't get any better in the second grade," another said. "Look at what his teacher wrote in the margin": 'Little Francisco, who would rather be called, 'Joe', wastes a lot of time in class telling dumb jokes.' And look at these high school transcripts. He barely squeaked through with a "B" average. His Civics teacher, Mrs. White, notes that 'Joe is not college material.'"

And just look at this newspaper article he wrote about a stripper in Mexico, another colonel piped in. Gadzooks, it has a picture of a nearly nude woman on the front page. Seems to me he was out carousing with his friends at strip joints instead of studying."

"Well, that settles it, this guy should be sent to the infantry," said the colonel.

"Wait a minute sir," said the West Pointer, "I see here he passed ROTC flight training and he has a private pilot's license."

"Yes, but take a look at the comment made by his instructor, Mr. Zeiss: 'Lewels is a real screw up.' What are we going to do with this piss-ant journalism major?"

The room fell silent. No one seemed to have a good idea. Then the West Pointer said, "Hey, I have an idea. Let's get him out of his comfort zone. If we send him to the Signal Corps or the Transportation Corps he will just cruise through the war just like he's been cruising through life. So let's put him in The Corps of Engineers, after all, we need more engineers." And that was that. It would be the engineers for me.

"Yes," I thought as I was driving through the mountains of West Virginia, "that's the way they did it. That had to be the way it went down. My past had come back to haunt me and now there was only one solution for me. I had to get smart fast and pass that darned engineer course, by hook or by crook. Maybe I could get the Cliff Notes somewhere."

ON the RIO GRANDE

16

Chapter *Diez y Seis*
Gaming the System

You can imagine how nervous I was on the first day of class at the U.S. Army Engineer Officer's Basic Course at Fort Belvoir, VA. There were 65 brand-new second lieutenants mingling at the back of the classroom and I overheard two of them talking. "Yeah, I went to M.I.T., how about you?" The other guy said, "That's cool, I went to Cal. Tech. Masters in Civil Engineering. Thinking of going for a Ph.D."

I knew I was in big trouble.

As the instructor entered the room, everyone scampered to find a seat and I snuggled into one on the last row, which was a long-engrained custom of mine. Our instructor was a tall, straight-backed major with several rows of ribbons on his chest. His uniform was heavily starched and pressed beautifully—not a wrinkle anywhere. I was glad I was on the back row where I could be as inconspicuous as possible. That way, he wasn't likely to point to me and say, "Lewels, calculate the square root of the hypotenuse of a right triangle squared, times the value of Pi," or something to that effect.

Instead, without saying a word, he turned to the chalkboard, picked up a piece of chalk and began writing what appeared to be some kind of complicated equation. It stretched from one end of the board to the other. Then he turned to the class and said. "Solve it."

Needless to say, I had no idea of what "it" was. As soon as he uttered the words, 64 slide rules came out of nowhere and the class began to diligently come up with the answer. As for me, I had never even held a slide rule or had any idea what one did. The thought of holding one in my hand made me nauseated. Besides, no one had mentioned to me prior to coming to class that slide rules would be necessary or that we should be sure to bring one with us. "Where do you even get one of those?" I wondered. "How did all those other guys know?" Then, it dawned on me. They all had degrees in engineering. I knew it. This was all a clever trap to get me to apply to flight school, and it looked as if it was going to work.

Seeing that my goose was cooked and I had no other alternative, I mustered the courage to raise my hand. A moment later the major towered over me. "What's the problem lieutenant?" he asked brusquely.

"Sir, I have a problem. There's been a big mistake. You see, I'm a journalism major and I was supposed to be assigned to the Intelligence Corps, but my orders got mixed up somewhere. I don't even know how to use a slide rule"

He looked down on me with a look of utter disgust, as if I was a cockroach or a sewer rat or maybe a liberal arts major. Finally, he said, "Well lieutenant, you can go see the commanding officer and request a transfer. But if you come back to this class you'd better have a slide rule and know how to use it." Then he turned and went back to the front of the class. I meekly picked up my notebook and pencil, stood up and crept out the back of the classroom. As I was leaving I heard the distinct sounds of snickering coming from various parts of the room.

"Boy," I thought. "Being the most famous kid in class on the first day is getting old and embarrassing." I had to figure out a fast way to outsmart the army. I was not looking forward to my next move. I had to go see the commanding officer and plead my case once again and it was not something I relished doing. I got in my car and drove to the headquarters building. I sat in my car taking a few deep breaths in preparation and thinking through my spiel, which by now I pretty much had down pat.

Soon, I was standing in front of a secretary's desk asking for an audience with a commanding officer. Apparently, he didn't have much to do that day, so she sent me right in. I stood at attention before him and saluted. He was seated at a large desk, cleared of any clutter. His office was wood paneled and decorated with citations and photos of himself with various generals and dignitaries. "Sir," I said while saluting, "lieutenant Lewels requesting permission to speak."

"At ease lieutenant," the colonel said without rising. "And by the way, we don't salute indoors in the army."

"Oh yes sir. Sorry sir."

By now I noticed that the commander bore a striking resemblance to F.B.I. director, J. Edgar Hoover, except he was uglier, if that was possible. He had a lower jaw that protruded sharply from his face, making him look like a bulldog. A mean bulldog. He had at least 15 rows of ribbons on his chest. It gave me a queasy feeling.

"Well, get on with it," he said, as if he had already heard every possible story there was to hear.

"Yes sir," I said. "Sir, there has been a terrible mistake. I was supposed to be assigned to the Intelligence Corps sir, but my orders got mixed up somewhere and I was assigned to the engineers by mistake. I'm sure it was just a clerical error. You see, I'm a journalism major and I don't know anything about engineering. I don't even have a slide rule. I want to request a transfer sir. You see, there was this form we were asked to complete in ROTC where we could choose from three different branches and…."

"Hold it there lieutenant," the bulldog interrupted. "Lieutenant, do you like that little gold bar on the collar of your uniform?" he asked. (The bar signified that I was a second lieutenant.)

"Yes sir, I do."

"You wouldn't like to see that gold bar turn into a gold stripe on your shirtsleeve, would you?" (That would have meant a demotion to private.)

"No sir."

"Well then, you'd better get your ass over to the Post Exchange (PX), buy yourself a slide rule and pass that course or else that is exactly what's going to happen," he shouted. I didn't get the feeling he was kidding.

In fact, I felt just like the lion in the Wizard of OZ after he met the wizard, got scared and ran for his life. I saluted, made a crisp about face and then nearly ran out of his office and all the way to the PX. "Wow," I thought, "what a pompous jerk. He wasn't in the least bit *simpatico* (pleasant). He could melt steel with that look. What am I going to do now?"

I sat in my car, recovering from the totally-uncalled-for ass chewing I had just received and tried to get my blood pressure under control. Then, I drove to the PX and asked a clerk where I could find a slide rule. Now for those of you who have no idea what a slide rule is, I will try to describe it. The slide rule was the calculator of its day. It looks like a ruler, but with a sliding device down the middle. The rule and the slide have numbers and hash marks all the way across that mark logarithmic scales. It is used for making quick calculations for multiplication, division, roots, logarithms and trigonometry. (I had to turn to Google for this description because I forgot it shortly after leaving engineer school.) Believe it or not, slide rules are such powerful calculating machines that they helped get our men into space. Modern hand calculators were invented in 1967, but they could only add, subtract, multiply and divide. The slide rule had an added benefit: it never ran out of battery power, because it didn't use batteries.

The one I bought at the PX came in a plastic, see-through carrying case and inside was a carefully-folded set of instructions. When opened fully, the paper was an 8X10 sheet with tiny instructions covering every inch of both sides. It made my blood run cold. I detested having to read instructions.

Anyway, slide rules were never used in any math classes I had ever taken. I didn't even know anyone who had one. Just the idea that I would have to read the instructions by myself and learn to operate it terrified me. I didn't even want to touch it.

However, I had no choice, so I bought it and took it back to my sparse bachelor's quarters. I sat down at the desk, turned on the desk lamp and started reading the instructions, trying hard not to barf all over them. Fortunately, they included sample problems that started out easy and got harder and harder. I opened my notebook and started working problems and taking notes. I stayed up all night practicing how to use the darn thing and, amazingly, by the next morning, I felt quite certain that I had become an engineer.

I went to class that day, kept my head down and barreled through eight weeks of holy hell. I did one other thing that day. I went back to the headquarters and got myself an application to the U.S. Army Aviation School. There was no way I was going to lead a platoon of engineers in battle after only eight weeks of training. However, I am quite proud to say that I passed that darned course and for the next three years I wore the castle insignia on my collar, denoting that I was a full-fledged officer in the U.S. Army Corps of Engineers. I never spent a day in an engineer unit, instead, I went to flight school, just as the army had wanted me to all along. However, I did learn some very useful skills during those eight weeks—skills that served me well for the rest of my life. I learned how to lay a mine field and how to remove a mine field (don't try this at home!). I learned how to build a bridge and how to blow it up, how to mix cement to army specifications, how to assemble and maneuver a pontoon boat through a swamp, how to blow up just about anything, and how to calculate the square root of the hypotenuse of a right triangle squared times the value of Pi (or something like that). Most importantly I learned that you don't need a stinking college education to be an engineer. All you need is a slide rule and eight weeks in the army.

Now I faced a new hurdle. I found out that nine out of ten applicants for flight school were assigned to helicopter training, regardless of which they requested. The problem was that I was a fixed-wing pilot and I wanted to make sure I didn't end up flying choppers. Choppers, as mentioned earlier, had a bad record of survival as they were used to fly into places that regular planes couldn't go because there were no airfields nearby. They flew into the jungle to unload or pick up ground troops and often the landing zones (LZs) were hot. That meant that the location was under enemy fire. Helicopter pilots had to hover in place in those hot LZs and wait for the passengers to unload or to load up. This, of course, made them sitting ducks. I had the greatest respect for the chopper pilots that flew in the Vietnam War. They were heroes and they all deserved numerous awards for their service to our country. I just didn't want to be one of them. Most of them had applied for fixed- wing training and been denied. Some of them just loved what they did.

By coincidence, there were 10 of us in the engineer class who had applied for flight school and the group got together to talk about the war and about what we could expect in aviation training. All ten of us wanted fixed-wing school. I could see there was a mathematical problem here. In all likelihood, nine of us would be disappointed. Maybe we all would be. This dilemma caused me to ponder the situation day and night as I stared at the application. I needed my application to stand out. But how? Then my imagination went to work. "Who," I wondered, "would make the decision and how would he make it?" I began to realize that all the applications looked the same. Therefore, whoever was responsible for the assignments, had no alternative but to make the assignments blindly. I could imagine a sergeant sitting at a desk at the Pentagon with a tall stack of applications and putting them in two stacks. Nine went into the helicopter training stack and one went into the fixed-wing stack. What else could he do? It must be the most boring job in the whole army.

Then, I realized that Fort Belvoir was only a short distance south of the Pentagon. Why hadn't I thought of that before? It was another of my "*gran idiotus!*" I decided that I would hand-carry my application directly to the

Pentagon and have a chat with that lonely sergeant. I even thought of taking him a bottle of Jack Daniels as a "gift", but then I thought that would look too much like bribery and dropped the idea. Actually, as I later learned how the army really works, I realized belatedly the bottle of booze would have been a great idea.

In any case, the first day I had off, I headed for the Pentagon, application in hand. As an army officer, I had easy access to that noble institution so I wandered the vast labyrinth of hallways until I found someone who actually knew something. What I found out was that I was in the wrong building. The man I was looking for was down the road at another army base. Fortunately, I still had time to drive over there and try to find the right office. It wasn't long before I found a cubicle manned by a major (apparently the job required a much higher level of brainpower) who wore wings on his chest and several ribbons. I deduced he was an army aviator who had recently returned from Vietnam. His assignment, boring as it was, was a necessary step up the ladder to an eventual promotion to lieutenant colonel. As I expected, he looked bored. On his desk was a large stack of papers—applications for flight school sent to him by officers from all over the country. There was a credenza behind his chair with a pot of coffee brewing. Perfect!

I stepped forward respectfully and introduced myself. "Major, I'm lieutenant Lewels and I'm considering applying for flight school. I was wondering if you had a moment to talk to me." I was careful to keep my application in my back pocket, so as not to make it obvious I was desperate.

He looked up at me from the newspaper he was reading and his broad smile told me I had hit pay dirt. "Sure lieutenant," he said amiably. "Have a seat. How about a cup of coffee?"

"Thank you very much major, I'll take mine black," I lied. I hated coffee, but if I ever had any, I would dilute it with plenty of milk and sugar. But not today. Today I was a tough member of the U.S. Army Corps of Engineers and applying for flight school was just something I had been mulling over. It was either flight school or a transfer to the infantry, I told him.

I could see he thought this quite admirable, but he advised me against the infantry. A man after my own heart! "No, no," he said. "You'll be much happier as an aviator, I assure you."

"I see from your ribbons that you've been to Vietnam. What did you fly over there?" I asked as I took a tiny sip of really strong and very bitter coffee.

"I was a Bird Dog pilot," he replied. "You know, reconnaissance."

"Oh yeah, I've heard about those. They're single-engine Cessnas, two seaters, isn't that right?"

"Yes, they are basically the same planes used in Korea. Now they are souped-up to 210 horsepower and they put variable-pitch props on them. They carry two rockets under each wing, two high explosives and two white phosphorous for marking targets," he explained.

"Oh, wow, I didn't know that," I said. "So what's it like over there flying a little Cessna?" I asked.

He was delighted to have someone, anyone, take an interest in him and his experiences in Vietnam. We gabbed for about an hour and he told me about all the times he had been shot at while flying low and slow over the jungle. "You know, you can't see through that thick jungle foliage unless you're right on top of the trees. But of course, that makes you really vulnerable," he explained. Then he told me about the friends he lost to enemy fire and those who went down and were never found. Some were presumed dead, but others were probably prisoners of war. All of a sudden becoming a fixed-winged aviator wasn't sounding so good. But neither was leading an engineer platoon. He could see that my enthusiasm was waning.

Finally, he said, "So how about it, are you going to apply for flight school?"

"Well, it sounds very exciting," I said, "but there is one problem."

"What's that?" the major said with a look of concern on his face?

"Well, I already have a private pilot's license and I feel that I would do a good job flying fixed-wing aircraft, like yourself. I'm just not sure I could handle helicopters. They're just not my cup of tea, if you know what I mean."

"Yeah, I know exactly what you mean," he said. "I'm with you there."

"I hear that most applicants to flight school are sent to helicopter training, is that right?" I asked.

"I'm afraid that's true. There's a shortage of helicopter pilots because of the high casualty rates. Also, the army is transitioning out of fixed-wing to rotary-wing craft. There's just a limited number of slots for fixed-wing school."

"Oh, that's a shame," I said. "I was kind of looking forward to being a pilot. So tell me major, how do you decide who flies choppers and who doesn't?"

"Well, just look at that stack of papers," he said, pointing to the large stack on his desk.

"Are all those applications for flight school?" I asked as if I hadn't thought of that before.

"Yes, exactly," he said. "And you know how I decide?"

"I have no idea."

"Well, since they all look alike, I just randomly put 9 into one stack and the tenth one goes into the fixed-wing stack," he confessed. With that, he reached over and took several of the completed applications from the top of the stack. "Here, take a look at these," he said, handing me the papers. "These are typical. These guys scribble their responses, misspell words and their writing is mostly illegible. It's hard to believe that they are officers."

Looking them over I could see what he meant. My own application didn't look much different. "I see what you mean," I said earnestly.

"They are a mess," he said. "And not only that, most all are requesting assignment to fixed-wing school."

"These are really depressing," I said in agreement. "I can see that my chances of getting into fixed-wing school are pretty slim."

"Well, wait a minute," he said. "Maybe there is something you can do to increase your chances."

"I don't understand," I said.

"What you need to do is make your application stand out."

"How would I do that?" I asked.

"When you send in your application, attach a letter to it. Here, I'll give you a blank application," he said as he reached in a drawer and handed me the paperwork. "Send it directly to my attention."

"Well, what should the letter say?" I asked.

"It should say that you're thinking of making the army your career and that becoming a fixed-wing aviator is part of your plan, in view of your previous flying experience. I would type it if I were you. Make it at least a couple of pages long," he advised. "Something like that might give you an edge," he hinted.

"Gee, major, thanks for the advice and for your time. I know you're a busy man," I said. I'll think it over. You've really been a great help to me and an inspiration."

We stood up and shook hands, and he wished me the best of luck in my career and I thanked him profusely for his attention. I drove back to Fort Belvoir, sat down at my typewriter and typed out my application. Then I wrote a four- page, single-spaced letter explaining in great detail my long-held desire to become an army fixed-wing aviator and to make the army my career. It was perhaps the best piece of fiction I had ever written—worthy of a budding new novelist. It may have been fiction, but it gave the major all the ammunition he needed to put my application in the right stack of papers. "If that's what it takes to outsmart the army, then so be it," I thought. Anyway, it wasn't as if the army had been honest, reasonable, or even sympathetic with me. Figuring out how to work the system to my advantage didn't seem so wrong. That's how you get ahead in this world. "You can't just sit back and hope things work out. You need to get smart and make the world work for you," I thought.

Graduation day for the Army's Engineer School was fast approaching and once again everyone in the class was anxious to learn about their new assignments. Many in the class had applied for all sorts of army schools and those of us who were going to flight school huddled together worrying about our futures. Finally the orders arrived and the instructor started calling out names. Eventually, everyone had his orders. Some were delighted, others were disappointed. "Oh God," one of my friends said. "I got chopper school." One by one, the flight school boys learned they were going to helicopter school. I opened my orders and, guess what? I was going to fixed-wing training—the only one of the ten.

When the others learned of my assignment, they were all huddled around me as if I were some kind of celebrity. "How did you get so lucky?" one asked. "Yeah," said another. "How did you do it?"

"Just the luck of the draw, I guess," I said. "I just got lucky." I felt bad for them, but I had learned a valuable lesson: sometimes you can't just wait around to be lucky, sometimes you have to make your own luck. I was beginning to think I was getting pretty smart, "the captain of my own ship," as they say. But the day was soon coming when I would seriously consider if that was true. In truth, I was just barely getting smart.

ON the RIO GRANDE

17

Chapter *Diez y Siete*
Dumb Luck?

My sister, Helen, always says, "That Joe, he is the luckiest guy. He can fall into a pile of crap and come out smelling like a rose!" And she's right. I seem to have lived a charmed life, getting into tight spots, many of them dangerous, and somehow getting through them unscathed. After my experiences in engineer school, I was beginning to think that luck had nothing to do with it. I just thought I was getting smarter.

Getting assigned to fixed-wing school was one of the first times I realized I was really getting smart. But the day I arrived at flight school I was greeted by a gruesome reminder that there was no safe way to get through the war. Just as I arrived at the headquarters to sign in, there was a terrible clatter just across the street at the base hospital. A Huey helicopter was landing on the helipad and several attendants came rushing out to take two soldiers on stretchers into the emergency room. That evening I found out they were already dead on arrival. They were the bodies of two student pilots who had just had a mid-air collision with each other. This event made a deep impression on me, as you might expect.

The war in Vietnam did not pose the only danger in my chosen career path. It turned out that student pilots are just as dangerous as teenage drivers, and this fact was born out in the statistics that we were made aware of when we arrived. There were so many fixed-wing and helicopter pilots being trained, due to the growing demand, that the night sky was alive with many dozens of aircraft's red and green running lights, all practicing nighttime maneuvers. On average, at the peak of the war, there were two fatalities per month related to pilot error or mechanical failures.

When I was there in training, we were told that Cairns Army Airfield at Ft. Rucker, Alabama, had more take-offs and landings each day than any other airport in the world. Night flying in formation with a bunch of student pilots was the scariest thing I ever did as an army aviator, aside from, of course, getting shot down in enemy territory in Vietnam. Among the many dangerous maneuvers we were required to accomplish was flying at night with ten or so other student pilots and making touch-and-go landings, one right behind the other, at a small airfield. All of this was done with very low lighting to mark the airstrip, simulating what we would find in Vietnam.

This was bad enough, but what made it worse was that another group of ten planes were doing the same thing on a parallel runway next to ours. Imagine 20 airplanes, flown by student pilots, flying around in circles in close proximity on a dark, moonless night under low lighting conditions. There were so many red tail lights bobbing up and down it was near impossible to keep track of which was which. Some of ours drifted over to their side and some of theirs drifted our way all night long. Whoever thought up this drill should have been court martialed.

I quickly began to believe I wasn't so smart after all. Serving in an engineer unit was beginning to look like a good option by my first week in flight school, even before we began our flying lessons. That was when we had our parachute training. The new arrivals stood in a long line where we were going to be issued our very own parachutes and our training. When it was my turn, a sergeant handed me a heavy parachute and instructed me on how to put it on.

"Just buckle that strap across your chest lieutenant and then bring the others between your legs and attach them to the other strap. Now, see that "D" ring on the left side of your chest? Okay, that's what you pull to open the chute. Just count to ten after you jump out of the plane and pull the "D" ring," he said with a wry smile.

"Okay, I got it," I said. "That's easy. When do we get to actually make our first jump?"

This question elicited a big laugh from the sergeant and his comrades who were standing around as if they were all in on a big joke.

"No jumps, lieutenant," he answered.

"What do you mean, no jumps?" I asked skeptically. "Don't we get to learn how to actually use these things?"

"Sir, you have just completed your parachute training," he said. "Please move along. We gotta keep the line moving."

I couldn't believe what he was saying. It made absolutely no sense. He had to be kidding.

"Wait a minute," I said. "There has to be more training. Where's the part where we learn how to hit the ground and roll when we land and stuff like that?" I asked.

"Lieutenant, "you're never going to have to do that," he answered with a laugh. The guys behind him thought this was hilarious.

"Well," I said logically, "If they're going to issue these to us they should teach us how to use them."

"Lieutenant," he said trying to clarify the bizarre information he had just given me. "Where you're going you'll never need that parachute. You're going to be flying at tree-top level. You'll be dead by the time you count to two," he said with a chuckle.

"Then why do they bother issuing these things? Why bother lugging these things around?" I asked with a little anger in my voice.

"Army regulations sir, just army regulations," he answered, as if he enjoyed watching the expression on the new lieutenants' faces when the reality set in.

I slowly began to see his point. But I still wasn't clear on one thing. "So what are we supposed to do with these things if we're never going to have to actually use them?"

"Well," he said, "most pilots just use them as back rests. No need to even strap them on."

It dawned on me that he was right. Learning how to actually use a parachute would have been a wasteful exercise. My job, the job of all reconnaissance pilots in Vietnam, was to observe enemy action on the ground. The problem was that you couldn't see anything through the dense jungle foliage. We Bird Dog pilots were the army's answer to today's drones. We were the eyes in the sky in Vietnam, but unlike the unmanned drones of today, which fly many thousands of feet in the air and use high-resolution cameras to scour the ground, mostly in desert environments, we had to fly low and slow to see anything. We flew at about 90 miles per hour with our windows open for air conditioning. Thanks to Uncle Sam, we got a front row seat to America's very unsuccessful war being fought in Southeast Asia.

As mentioned earlier, aviation school was nine months long and we were all hoping the war would be over by the time we graduated. However, that was not the case. Instead, the U.S. was sending more troops and more equipment to Vietnam than ever before. Upon graduation, we all received orders to join units either already engaged in the war or new units just forming up and getting ready to go. My orders instructed me to report to the 203rd Reconnaissance Airplane Company (RAC) at Fort Sill, Oklahoma, which would be shipping out soon. This is where I discovered that aviation units were unique in that aviators were all officers and therefore, a company-sized unit would have about 20 pilots as well as a commanding officer

(CO) and an Executive Officer (XO). All the others, mechanics, clerks and such were enlisted men or non-commissioned officers (NCOs).

The "gung-ho" officers were tripping all over themselves to get one of the miscellaneous jobs needed to keep the unit running smoothly. Those wanting to further their careers, mostly regular army types, unlike reserve officers like myself, battled to get a job. I sat back and watched as they all vied for jobs such as supply officer, scheduling officer or some other paper-pushing jobs that freed up the CO and the XO to spend more time at the officer's club. I held back until the CO asked if anyone wanted to be the unit's public information officer (PIO). No one wanted the job because it was a piddly-ass job that led nowhere as far as a military career was concerned. Because I was the only one with a journalism background, I raised my hand and without further ado, I became the unit PIO on the spot, a position that I later discovered had many subtle benefits.

Vietnam was simultaneously enchanting and mysteriously foreboding. My unit's area of operation was bordered by the South China Sea to the east and the Cambodian border to the west. It was a paradise of lush jungle, cloud-covered mountains and fertile plains, where men plowed their rice paddies by hand, using wooden plows pulled sluggishly by water buffalo. It was called the "Central Highlands" and it covered an area approximately 100 miles wide and 350 miles long.

As our chopper came in to deliver us to our tiny base near a village called Phu Hiep, I could see that my new home featured a short airstrip pointing toward the white, sandy beach and the turquoise waters of the sea. The south side was shared by a CH-47 "Chinook" company, two UH-1 "Huey" chopper units, and several fixed-wing units, including our own Bird-Dog company. On the north side of the runway stood a large field hospital, buzzing with medevac helicopters bringing in the wounded and the dead from the battles raging not far away. The entire base was enclosed with barbed wire and mine fields, which gave me the feeling of being only semi-safe.

It was only later, as I began flying missions far into those mysterious, cloud-covered mountains that the war began to be all too real. People were shooting at me! At first the bullets sounded like bumble bees whizzing past the cockpit, but then they sounded like a sledge hammers when they hit the plane. That really got my attention, and it was hard not to take it personally. My job was to find the enemy and call in airstrikes on their positions. However, about the only way to find the enemy in the dense-jungle foliage was when they shot at me. So, basically, the job of the Bird Dog pilot was to go out and get shot at, which is what we did every day.

The instructors at the army aviation school had neglected to tell us that our job in Vietnam was to be bait! Upon arrival in Vietnam, we were instructed to call in airstrikes on any target from which we received enemy fire, even if the shots came from a village that had women and children. As far as the army was concerned, they were all "gooks" and considered to be the enemy. This didn't ring true with me. After all, the people of the Central Highlands were just peasant farmers. It didn't seem to me they cared which way the war went; they just wanted to grow their rice and be left alone. They were caught in the middle, between the Viet Cong and the U.S. Army—between the struggle between communism and capitalism. Looking down at the people in their black pajamas and coolie hats I wasn't at all certain that they knew the difference. In short, I very quickly discovered I had a developed a new philosophy: I had grave doubts about killing people I didn't even know and I vowed not to do it unless it was to protect our troops on the ground.

After the first few weeks of flying combat missions, I just couldn't call in airstrikes if there were civilians down there. If you ever saw a village being napalmed from close proximity I think you would feel the same way. What was even worse was that our job was to fly in super low, after the strike had obliterated the foliage, and to count the number of charred bodies, including women and children.

"How many gook bodies down there?" called the fighter pilot who had just delivered the napalm. I was never sure. Did half a gook count as much as a full gook? How about a leg or an arm? What about a charred, bloody mess that could be a dog or part of a water buffalo? In the end, I would just make up a number. "It looks like 15 KIA," I would report. But I knew that wouldn't be a satisfactory answer.

"Go back down and count again," the fighter pilot would order. Amazingly, on the second pass I found another ten fictitious bodies. "Make that 25 KIA," I reported. "Okay, good work. Over and out," the faceless voice would announce, the jet long out of sight.

The body count was then passed up the chain of command. "The more bodies the better," was their motto. Progress in the war was pinned to the daily, weekly and monthly body counts and this information was passed on to the American public every night on the evening news. It made me sick.

Many of our troops also took to referring to all Vietnamese people as "gooks," or "slopes," not just the enemy. But I never could. It was a terribly racist thing to do, but I realized it was their way of absolving themselves of the horrors they were committing on a regular basis. By using these racial slurs, they convinced themselves that the people they were killing were less than human. Maybe it was because of my experience with racism that I refused to speak about the Vietnamese people that way. In fact, I went out of my way to become friendly with those who worked on the base. I was even invited regularly to dine with them in their homes where they served their favorite dishes of fermented fish heads, other things I didn't recognize, rice and, thankfully, lots of beer. The people I got to know were kind, gentle and gracious, and they did not deserve to be looked upon as a lower class, or sub-human.

By the time my tour was over, I saw my share of combat. I was shot at and I was shot down. I had to make emergency landings in tiny airstrips and I had close calls with death way too many times. I had to fly my small plane through a typhoon at night; I got caught in bad weather frequently; and I survived them all through what I thought was blind luck. But was it luck? I was forced to consider other possibilities when something very strange happened to me on what I believed to be a quite ordinary day.

ON the RIO GRANDE

18

Chapter *Diez y Ocho*
The Hole

Have you ever had an experience that was so amazing and bizarre that it changed your entire perception of reality? That's what happened to me one lovely day as I was flying my small plane in the mountains of the Central Highlands.

Just describing what it was like to fly alone over endless jungle during wartime is difficult. On the one hand, it was so serene and beautiful that when I wasn't being shot at, it was an amazingly peaceful and even surreal experience. Troops of monkeys could often be seen flittering through the tree tops, waterfalls frequently burst forth from the mountainsides, plunging to the valley floor and small hamlets of thatched-roof huts built on stilts would suddenly appear in a small clearing. These were home to the indigenous tribespeople who often found themselves caught up in a war they barely understood. Because I had to fly low through the valleys, surrounded by mountain peaks towering on all sides, I was often out of radio contact with anyone. Being alone like that gave me a sense of freedom I had never known before. Maybe that's why I wanted to be a pilot. Up there no one could give me orders. I was my own boss much of the time, and there was no other job like it. However, at the same time, there was also the thrill of knowing that the peacefulness could be interrupted at any moment. If you let yourself think about it, the very real danger of your situation would start to work on your mind, causing your muscles to tighten and your mouth to get dry.

Cruising just above the thick jungle below was like being in a time machine that took me back to the Stone Age. The heat and humidity rising from the jungle floor filled the cockpit with the faint odor of vegetation that grew in great abundance in the valleys and on the mountainsides. For mountain pilots the dangers were much different than for those flying in the Mekong River Delta in the southern portion of Vietnam. A small plane in the mountains didn't have the horse power to climb quickly if the elevation of a nearby mountain was misjudged. It was easy to get distracted and to fly up a valley that suddenly ended. Sometimes there wasn't time to make a quick U turn, and that's how some planes went down.

And then there was the weather. Clouds and storms could sweep in unexpectedly from the South China Sea and the visibility could drop suddenly. As much as I wanted to relax and enjoy an experience that few people ever get to have, I could never take my attention away from the many dangers all around, not the least of which was unexpectedly becoming the target of enemy fire. Staying focused meant staying alive.

It was on one of these lonely sojourns through the mountains one day that I found myself flying south, parallel to the Cambodian border, on my way to a tiny outpost to deliver some documents and to pick up their mail. It was a beautiful day and the jungle seemed unusually alive, a color of deep green I haven't seen elsewhere. I landed at the tiny strip, had a cup of coffee (with cream and sugar), concluded my business, and I was off again, this time due east toward my base on the seashore.

It was only about 100 miles from the border to the ocean, but between the two lay 5,000-foot peaks and numerous valleys where there was the possibility of finding enemy encampments. Even though I was well-trained in instrument flying, the rule was to try not to get caught in instrument conditions due to the fact that the navigation aids normally used for instrument flying in the states simply were not as sophisticated in Vietnam, particularly for low-flying aircraft.

On this particular day I decided to just follow the road that led through the mountains, directly toward the coast. It was routine. The flight would last about an hour and twenty minutes, depending on headwinds, under normal conditions. But about 30 minutes into my flight I began to see clouds cascading over the tops of the mountains and beginning to sweep down into the valley. All too soon, the fast-moving front blocked the mountain pass directly in my path and the ceiling was dropping fast. I had no choice; I had to turn around and go back to Ban Me Thuot, the outpost where I had just been. But, when I turned, I realized I was boxed in. The low-hanging clouds and lots of rain caused the visibility to suddenly drop to zero. The surrounding mountains disappeared in the cloud banks, and suddenly I was in a "whiteout" condition. Flying blindly through the mountains was not an option; l had but one alternative. I had to go up.

I was in a jam. With no visibility, I turned to my instruments and guided my aircraft in a slow circle, climbing up, up and way up. There was no way to know where the tops of the clouds would be. It could be a few thousand feet or it could be 20,000 feet, but I had no choice but to keep climbing. Finally, at just above 10,000 feet I broke out of the clouds into bright sunshine and I quickly saw what the weather had brought me. The top of the cloud layer was flat and stretched in all directions as far as the eye could see. There were no giant thunderheads, like the kind we get back home in West Texas, that bring with them lightning and thunder. No, this was a monsoon, the kind that lingers for days and pours down buckets of water in a matter of hours. This was not good. The good news was that I would not need oxygen at that altitude, even though some might suffer altitude sickness if they weren't accustomed to living in the mountains. I, however, had often gone skiing at altitudes higher than this and suffered no ill effects, so that wasn't a worry. Besides, our planes were not equipped with oxygen.

The problem was I couldn't risk going back down through the clouds with mountains below. Another problem was that my small plane did not have sophisticated instruments designed for instrument flying, such as radar or a transponder, which would allow air-traffic controllers to monitor my position. My altitude did, however, allow me to tune in to the radio frequencies of the air bases within my cruising range. The radio chatter told me the airports were closed. That ruled out an attempt at an instrument-guided approach. It was clear that I would have to find my own way down.

I knew I was in trouble, but the bright sunshine and the beautiful blanket of snow-white clouds just below somehow gave me a sense of well-being. So I did the only thing I could do; I steered a course directly eastward, toward the coast and I started looking for breaks in the clouds. There were none. To determine my location relative to the coast, I tuned one of my directional radios to a station I knew was precisely on the oceanfront, the Tuy Hoa airbase, just north of my home base. The needle on my instrument, which now pointed almost due east, would gradually begin turning to my left as I approached the beach.

I flew along like this for nearly 40 minutes, hopping along with my wheels brushing the clouds below and searching desperately for an opening in the carpet of white. It looked like it covered the entirety of South Vietnam and the South China Sea, so the hopes of finding a way down were diminishing quickly. And I only had about an hour and a half of fuel left in my tanks. I couldn't stay up there forever.

I began to devise a plan that might work, but only if the visibility would improve in the next hour or so. I thought I could go past the coast for maybe 20 minutes or so and then begin a slow descent through the clouds on instruments and then, hopefully, see the ocean in time to level out. Then I would turn back toward land and find my way back to my base. It would be risky. If visibility was so bad that the airbases had to shut down, then my hopes of pulling up short of the water were not good.

Of course there was always the parachute. I thought about it, but then I remembered my parachute training. I was pretty sure I would be able to count to ten before pulling the D ring, but where would I land? The mountains would not be a good option and neither would the ocean. I had not been issued a flotation device even though we often flew over the sea. I reviewed my survival training in my mind. At Ft. Rucker we had to pass an "escape and evasion" course during which we had to run through the Alabama thickets at night with a bunch of fake Viet Cong chasing us. If we got caught we would be taken to a "POW camp" and endure several hours of heavy interrogation. Then they would take us back to the start and we had to run for our lives once again, evading the enemy and reaching a safe post, several miles away. Our only aids were a flashlight, a map, and a compass for navigation. The enemy was made up of a special unit of U.S. soldiers who were trained to scare the wits out of us and make the experience seem very real.

When I inevitably got caught, the camp was full of captives, all being verbally abused and made to trudge through a pit of mud up to their waists. Others were stripped down to their shorts and tied to wooden posts; they were made to believe they were going to be whipped.

In the enemy command post, each "prisoner" had his opportunity to be interrogated by a big "enemy" officer who would sit him at a table, shine a bright light in his face, and then, sitting face to face, he would be yelled at and cursed. These guys took their jobs seriously. And it's a good thing they did because the experience had the desired effect. Going down in the jungle and being captured was just not an option. I would sooner crash into the ocean. After all, we all knew what the Viet Cong did to Bird Dog pilots whenever they got their hands on one. There would be days of endless torture and then a gruesome death. They were known to drag the bodies of pilots from village to village to display them for the people to see, then they would hang the body from a tree and let it rot. We had all heard stories of even worse outcomes so gruesome that I won't mention them here.

No, parachuting into the jungle was not an option I would consider. However, if it happened that I found myself in such a situation, I had a number of items with me that might help me survive. I carried an M-1 carbine rifle, which was lightweight and accurate up to about 100 yards. I also carried a sawed-off 12- gauge shotgun for close combat. It was ideal if it came to a fight in the close-quarters of a jungle environment. The army required that we carry a 45-caliber pistol, which was in a holster on my right hip. It was not required, but it was recommended that we carry a 12-inch Bowie knife, which I carried on my left hip. Every pilot had been issued a flak vest which had a ¾ inch thick steel plate that fit in a sleeve on the chest. But since most of the bullets coming at us were from below, we just slid the armored plate under our seat cushion, which gave us a feeling of great comfort. I had also scrounged a couple of hand grenades. If it came to jungle survival, I wasn't going down without a fight, and I didn't plan on getting captured. As for my skills in hand-to-hand combat, well, I had none. Believe it or not, that was not part of the curriculum in flight school.

My other survival gear included matches in a water-proof container, an emergency radio, water-purification tablets, malaria pills, a mirror for signaling, and a few other odds and ends. Reviewing my gear only made me that much more certain that I was not going to go down over land. I would rather swim and take my chances with the sharks.

You might wonder why I didn't make contact with my base at this point. And that is a good question. First of all, there was nothing they could do to help me and secondly, I wasn't supposed to be up this high. Thirdly, we were not supposed to fly on instruments. I just couldn't find a good reason to make the call. I started the day at another base where I spent the night, so they hadn't heard from me all day. Since they weren't hailing me on the radio, they must be thinking I am on the ground somewhere safe. No need to upset the applecart if it's not completely necessary. Of course, if I had to bail out or in the event I tried flying down through the clouds towards the sea, I would let everyone know. But I was not there yet.

I kept scanning the tops of the clouds and praying for a break while at the same time scanning my instruments, checking my navigational radio and my fuel gauge. I couldn't find even the smallest break in the monsoon, but the radio needle was beginning to point due north, indicating I was getting close to the shoreline. When the needle pointed directly to my left, I would know I was very close to shore, but the radio needle wouldn't tell me how close to the beach I was because the shoreline wasn't a straight line. It was a jagged and curving line and there were places where the mountains dropped straight into the ocean, creating 200-300 foot cliffs. The one thing the needle would tell me for certain, however, was that if I flew due east for another 15 or so minutes, I would be clear of the mountains and most likely over water.

Finally, the needle was pointing north, where the air base beacon was located. I had to decide what to do. It was then that I noticed something quite remarkable. In the ocean of white clouds below me, I saw what looked like a hole in the clouds a few hundred meters to my right. I quickly decided to go check it out. When I reached it, I was shocked. It was a perfectly round hole, about 50 yards in diameter. As I flew above it, I could see that it went down all the way, 10,000 feet, straight to the ground. Even more amazingly, I could clearly see the waves breaking on the beach far below. In all of my flying career, I had never seen a perfectly round hole in the clouds. Clouds are always moving around and they don't hold their shape very long, yet, I didn't give it another thought. Somehow I knew the hole was for me. Someone or something had opened another door for me and it wasn't for me to question.

I immediately put the plane into a steep, spinning dive and I plunged straight down toward the beach. I don't know how long I was in that amazing tunnel, but it seemed like an eternity. The entire time I was diving I kept watching the wall of the hole to make sure it wasn't closing in on me, then I would look down to make sure the coastline was still visible, and then I would check my airspeed to make sure I didn't over-rev the engine and cause it to blow. My eyes kept darting back and forth: the clouds, the shore, the airspeed, over and over. I calculate it took about two to three minutes to dive those 10,000 ft.

I probably wouldn't be writing these words if the hole had closed up on me in the middle of my dive, but remarkably it held its shape all the way down. When I finally reached the ground, I pulled the nose up and saw that I had less than 200 feet of visibility under the cloud layer, barely enough to fly over the waves, north to my base. But before I did that, I had to take one more look at that hole. I circled around and looked up through the Plexiglas window above me, just in time to see the hole close up. I had made it with only seconds to spare.

What do you call an experience like that? Is it a miracle or just dumb luck? I'm not sure I know. Anyway, I turned north, I called in to my unit's operations room to let them know I was coming in, and within 15 minutes I was landing at the small strip at Phu Hiep that I called home. I taxied off the runway and over to the parking area where I began to chock the tires and to tie-down the plane. Before I could finish I was surrounded by the ground crew, whose job it was to secure the plane and refuel it. To say they were surprised to see me would be an understatement. Mine was the only plane to have taken off or landed that day. When I reported in to the operations office, my CO and several pilots were waiting. They were on me immediately. "Where have you been?" the CO asked.

"Ban Me Thuot, sir. I picked up the mail," I said, as I put the packet on the desk.

"You flew here from the Cambodian border in this weather?" he queried. I could see the skepticism on his face.

"Yessir," I said.

"We've been socked in all day. No one has been able to take off or land.

In fact the field is closed. All the fields are closed."

"Gee, I didn't know," I said.

"Why didn't you call in your location?" he asked.

"I didn't think I needed to; I filed a flight plan." I answered nonchalantly.

"So how did you make it through the mountains in the middle of a monsoon?" he asked.

"No problem, Sir" I said. "Easy-peasy."

They all looked at me with a combination of skepticism and puzzlement. They knew it wouldn't have been easy flying through the monsoon, but they couldn't deny that I was standing there in front of them. I just smiled, turned and nonchalantly headed to the officer's club. I saw no reason to explain. They wouldn't believe me anyway. Better they thought I was the world's greatest aviator than a liar or a weirdo.

Second Lieutenant, Joe Lewels (age 23), is shown here at Phu Hiep, Republic of South Vietnam, with his Bird Dog, reconnaissance airplane in November, 1967. The Bird Dog was a single-engine Cessna used for low-level flight over the jungles of the Asian nation to detect enemy activity in support of ground troops. The jungle was so dense that the way the enemy was detected was when they began shooting at the tiny plane. Lewels writes that "The army never told us that our job was to be bait."

19

Chapter *Diez y Nueve*
What the Heck is Tet?

By early January, 1968, I had been flying missions for about three months when I found myself delivering hometown news releases to the Public Information Officer at our high command, the 17th Combat Aviation Group headquarters in the beautiful coastal city of Nha Trang. Up until then I had not actually thought there might be a way to get an assignment that would not include dropping bombs on people. But that's when I met the Group PIO.

Captain Heydeman was a chopper pilot who had been appointed the Group PIO because he had worked as a journalist in the states. He invited me to lunch at the Groups's semi-plush, air conditioned, officer's club, and after some light chit chat, he said, "I'm looking for my own replacement. My tour of duty is up and the Group needs to find someone with the right qualifications for the job. The job requires an aviator who also has a background in journalism."

"Well," I said, trying not to seem too excited, "I have a degree in journalism and I worked my way through school working for a public relations company and an ad agency in my junior and senior years. I also wrote for the school paper," I added.

Heydeman eyes lit up. "You're exactly what we're looking for!" he said excitedly. "How would you like to take over my job when I leave next week?" he asked.

"Well, it sounds good to me, but I don't think my CO would be too happy about losing one of his pilots. I don't think he would let me take the job."

"Just leave that to me," he said with confidence. "When you get back to your unit, pack your stuff and be ready to go. I'll have a chopper come pick you up. My boss outranks your boss, so there won't be any trouble."

The next afternoon I was called to our company's operation room at Phu Hiep. Major Stevenson, the CO, was in a rage. "What the hell did you do Lewels?"

I played dumb. "What do you mean, major," I said innocently.

"I just got a call from Group headquarters. They say they're sending a chopper for you and for you to get your gear out to the airstrip, now!"

"Oh, wow," I said. "All I did was have lunch with Captain Heydeman when I was in Nha Trang. He's the outgoing PIO for the Group. He said he needed a replacement, but it wasn't like I was applying for the job."

"Well, apparently you did," he said with a scowl on his face. "Pack your bags and get the hell out of here."

Boy he was mad. He thought I had gone over his head, but I assured him I hadn't. "It was just an accidental meeting," I explained. He didn't care. He was losing one of his pilots and it would be some time before he could get a replacement. As for me, I followed orders, gathered my gear and ran to the airfield where my chopper was waiting. It took about 20 minutes to get to Nha Trang and Captain Heydeman was waiting to escort me to my new, much nicer, quarters and to show me my new office. I could tell he was greatly relieved to have found a replacement. Now he could go home knowing he wasn't leaving his boss in a lurch. I couldn't have been happier. Finally, my skills as a journalist would be put to use in the army. It had been a roundabout way, but somehow it had happened. "Just dumb luck, once again," I thought. "Or was it?"

But just to be clear, my flying duties had only been slightly diminished. As Group PIO I became editor of the group's newspaper, *The Eagle's Talons*, which required me to fly out to our outlying units on a regular basis. I was also assigned several combat missions each month, but far fewer than before. My new job was less dangerous, but flying in a small airplane anywhere in Vietnam, for any reason, was a dangerous endeavor. A small oil leak, or some such thing, that could easily be repaired on the ground, could be catastrophic if it happened in the air over enemy territory, and everywhere was enemy territory.

It was in my capacity as the Group's PIO that I found myself in Saigon at the end of January, delivering a stack of news releases to higher headquarters. By coincidence, I had been invited to attend a big party in celebration of the Vietnamese Lunar New Year (called Tet), given by a pilot who flew for a civilian airline called Air America. It was common knowledge that this organization was a front for the CIA. He was just one of numerous, interesting characters I got to know in the war.

This CIA guy had a big apartment in Saigon, which at the time was the party-capital of Southeast Asia. The nightlife there was exciting as Americans mingled with people from around the world in the busy restaurants and even busier cabarets and bars. The central area of town was lit up like Times Square in New York and the streets were jammed with pedestrians into the wee hours of the night. As a pilot with access to an airplane, I had many opportunities to travel the country, and when I wasn't flying combat missions, Saigon was the place to go.

The night of the big party, on January 31, 1968, all the partygoers were dressed in civilian clothes and there were members of the various services in attendance, as well some American nurses and secretaries who worked for the Department of Defense. The booze was flowing and the music was blaring, until finally around three in the morning the party started to break up. The CIA guy was going to take some of the ladies back to their apartment, so I hitched a ride with them back to my hotel. It was at that precise moment that the North Vietnamese Army launched its most aggressive campaign against the major cities of the south. It was called "The Tet Offensive." By chance, I was in Saigon the night it started and I was a witness to some of the heaviest fighting the war had seen. But that's not the end of the party story.

Those of us who had been at the party, as well as those who were still there, were oblivious to the attack that was raging on the outskirts of Saigon. Nor did we know that the Vietnamese government was enforcing a curfew that started several hours earlier. There were six of us in the CIA guy's Citroen automobile, three men and three women. However, we were not aware that our driver had way too much to drink and should not have been driving. That fact became apparent soon after pulling away from his apartment. Not only was he driving wildly, but it was then we realized something in the city had changed. The city was dark. All the buildings had gone dark as had the street lights. When we approached the first major intersection we noticed barricades blocking all entrances, except for a narrow passage for the authorities.

South Vietnamese military police carrying M-16 semi-automatic weapons were guarding each of the barricades. The CIA guy blew past them as if they weren't even there. Then we came upon another barricaded intersection and once again our leader screeched around them without so much as a wave at the guards. Finally, the girls said, "Here's our building," so the driver pulled to the curb, allowing them to exit the car and run into the darkened doorway to their quarters. Now there were just the three men left in the car.

Just then, as we were pulling away, three Jeeps full of South Vietnamese soldiers screeched to a halt and blocked us in. They were out of their Jeeps and on us before we had a chance to think. I was pulled roughly out of the car and slammed against the side door, the muzzle of a rifle placed firmly on the back of my head. I could see the same was happening to the other two. The M.P.s were jabbering away in Vietnamese and even though I had no idea what they were saying, I could tell they weren't happy. In fact, they were very angry, and they were making their point by shoving their weapons into our backs. To them, we were just criminals who had violated their curfew in a very disrespectful way. In no time we were handcuffed and shoved into Jeeps, each of us into a different Jeep. Their leader, who spoke some English, said, "You violate curfew! You going to jail."

It was at that moment that I had my first clear thought. "I'm an American officer," I yelled. "I demand to be taken to the American officer jail." (I had no idea if there was such a place, but I thought it was worth the try.)

Thankfully, that got their attention. "You got I.D.?" the leader asked. "Yes, it's in my back pocket," I said. With that, he uncuffed me and allowed me to show him my military I.D. He scrutinized it carefully, shining his flashlight on it for a long time. Finally, he said, "Okay, lieutenant, you going to American jail." And off we went. I don't know where the other two were taken, but I was pretty sure it wasn't going to be as nice as where I was going.

After a short ride we arrived at the Vietnamese jail, not the American jail as I had been told. I was put into a cell by myself and I immediately started raising hell. "This isn't the American jail." I yelled. "I want to see an American officer." These demands finally got their attention and they began discussing my fate amongst themselves. It was obvious they didn't want to let me go. Finally, they made a call and about 30 minutes later, an American M.P arrived. He had two stripes on his arm. He was a corporal, not an officer, and he stood about five foot tall. He ambled up to my cell with a big smirk on his face, as if he was enjoying the scene immensely. We looked at each other through the bars for a few moments and then I began to say, "Boy am

I glad to see you," but he interrupted me and said, "I hate officers."

I was at a complete loss for words. I had to do some quick thinking. Finally, after a very long moment of silence, I said, "I hate officers too. I really hate officers. I wanted to be an enlisted man, like you, but my father made me take ROTC in college. I'm with you corporal. Officers are horrible people." I babbled on like this for a couple of minutes, but I could tell he wasn't buying it.

My babbling did, however, elicit a reluctant smile. A small one. He turned without a word and walked away to speak to the Vietnamese M.P.s. After about ten minutes of what seemed to be an argument, the corporal came back to me and said, "Okay, lieutenant, this is your lucky day. They're going to let me take you to the American jail, but they want to follow us to make sure I'm not just going to let you go. Understand?"

"Yeah, sure," I said. "I understand."

"They want to walk in with us and watch me lock you up again," he added.

"Okay," I said. "Let's go."

When we got to the other jail and when the Vietnamese M.P.s were certain I was locked away, they finally left. As soon as they were gone, an American M.P. captain came over to my cell, unlocked it and let me out. "So lieutenant, why were you out on the streets after curfew. Don't you know Saigon is under attack?"

"Saigon is under attack?" I questioned. "No, I didn't know. I was at a New Year's party that started this afternoon. No one said anything about a curfew or an attack."

"Where are you stationed?" he asked.

"Nha Trang," I answered. "I'm here on official business for the 17th Combat Aviation Group."

"Okay, then," he said, apparently satisfied that I wasn't a North Vietnamese spy. "Where are you staying?"

"I'm at the Caravelle Hotel downtown," I answered.

"Okay," he said, "Let's go. I'll give you a ride."

It was still dark by the time I got to my hotel and I could hear the sound of artillery fire and machine-gun fire not so far away. I thanked the captain and immediately made my way to the rooftop terrace of the hotel where I could clearly see the war taking place only a few miles away. One of the enemy's objectives was the air base where my plane and firearms were stowed, so I spent the next few days encamped with several dozen other hotel guests watching the progress of the invasion. Because there was a restaurant and bar on the roof, we spent the time eating steaks, drinking scotch and listening to the news on the radio. The attack came as a total surprise because no one had ever believed the enemy could get so close to the capital city of Saigon with such a large force. We had no way of knowing if the fighting would make its way downtown and to the hotel. Our only solution was to drink more scotch. Thankfully, we did not have to resort to hand-to-hand combat, using only our steak knives for defense.

The Tet Offensive of 1968, launched by 84,000 North Vietnamese soldiers and Viet Cong guerillas against the major cities of the South, was the turning point in the war. The North was not successful in taking any of its major objectives, but those of us trapped in Saigon didn't know it at the time. Fierce fighting continued for several days, but before the enemy forces were repelled, they managed to attack the Presidential Palace and temporarily seize the American Embassy. Further north, the enemy had attacked my home base at Nha Trang, and had nearly overrun a large Marine base called Khe San, which beame one of the deadliest battles of the war. In desperation, the Marines called in B-52 air strikes, within close proximity of their own positions, to repel the overwhelming force.

However, even though the attacks ultimately failed, the Tet Offensive became a public relations victory for the North. More and more Americans turned against the war as they realized they had been fed a stream of lies about how well we were doing and how it was just a matter of time before we won.

Tet signified we were not winning and that we were not in control. The demonstrations back home intensified. American soldiers returning home were spat upon and called "baby killers" by anti-war protestors. Instead of being honored for the sacrifices they made for their country, they had to hide the fact they had ever been in Vietnam. It was a hard pill to swallow. But, for those of us who were there, the truth was quite clear. The Vietnamese were determined to win at all costs, even to the last man standing. The American troops had no such convictions. Every U.S. soldier I knew had a calendar next to his bed and he marked a big "X" for every day that he survived. Our troops were there for one-year tours and each man knew exactly how many days he had left before he was going home. It was clear to me that the North had the psychological advantage. They were willing to live in underground tunnels for years if they had to. The U.S. troops were not. I knew I certainly wasn't. We were not winning the war and no amount of bombing would change that. Even so, it took another seven years for the politicians to admit defeat and start recalling our troops. In all, more than 58,000 Americans died fighting a war that was ill-conceived and poorly carried out. In later years, it was revealed that our top brass knew our cause was hopeless, even as they sent more young Americans to their deaths (not to mention the million and a half Vietnamese soldiers and civilians who perished.)

As for me, I miraculously survived my tour and I came back to an unappreciative public in late October, 1968. By then, the army had promoted me to the rank of captain and I had been awarded the Bronze Star and the Air Medal for serving my country in combat during the war in the Republic of South Vietnam. (If I had known ahead of time that I was going to survive, I would have tried to enjoy it a bit more.)

It's clear I was no hero. From the beginning, my goal was to not get killed and to not hurt or kill others. Unfortunately that was not possible. For many years I didn't like talking about my year in Vietnam, but today, if anyone asks me, "Were you in Vietnam?" I always answer, "Damn right I was in 'Nam! I was in Saigon the night the Tet Offensive started. It was holy hell!"

The Bird Dog—The Army Observation-1 (O-1), single-engine Cessna, flying in the II Corps area of the Republic of South Vietnam. 1967.

ON the RIO GRANDE

20

Chapter *Veinte*
Losing My Cool

I must digress here and go back to my days at Burges High School when I became "cool" while passing for Anglo, due to my non-Mexicany last name and with a little help from my older sister. Being seen as one of the "cool" boys gave me self-confidence and made those years quite enjoyable.

However things changed very quickly when I enrolled in college in the fall of 1962. This is when I learned a harsh lesson: coolness doesn't transfer. I discovered that you can't count on being cool in college just because you were once cool in high school, and that came as quite a shock to me. My lesson began when some my friends and I decided to go through fraternity rush week at Texas Western College. Some of our older friends who were already in fraternities encouraged us to attend the rush parties held by the different Greek fraternities for the purpose of recruiting the cool incoming freshmen. At the end of rush week the bids would be made to the newcomers via sealed envelopes to be picked up in the union building. We had friends who were encouraging us to sign up to join Kappa Sigma, which was known more for their parties than for their elitism.

On the day when the bids were made, I went to the union building to pick up my envelope and found that it was empty. I had received no bids, not even from the Kappa Sigs. Several of my friends did get bids, so I was a bit puzzled as to what had happened. However, since I was taking a full load of 18 credit hours and I was working a full-time job, I decided it wasn't a big deal. I wouldn't have the time to invest in a fraternity anyway. I thought maybe that was the reason I didn't get in. However, the following week I ran into one of the Kappa Sigs who had been urging me to go through rush and he stopped me to have a little chat.

"I'm so sorry about what happened," he said.

"Oh, that's okay," I said, "It's no big deal."

"No, you don't understand. You should have gotten in, but there was one guy who blackballed you."

"You mean it only takes one 'no' vote to blackball someone?" I asked skeptically.

"Yeah," he said. "The way we do it is that everyone has a deck of cards and then when a nominee's name comes up each member throws a card onto the floor. Red means 'yes,' and black means 'no'. When your name came up they were all red until this one guy threw down a black card and said, 'Mexican.'"

"You mean I was blackballed because I'm Mexican? Is that allowed?"

"Sure," he said. "A guy can get blackballed for anything, and it takes a unanimous vote to get in."

"That's crazy," I said. "I had no idea it was that way. So are there Mexicans in any of the fraternities?"

"No, I don't think so," he said, ashamedly. "Mexicans aren't usually accepted. But you don't look Mexican and your name isn't Mexican, so I never thought that would be a problem."

"So who was it?" I asked.

"Sorry, I can't say," he said sheepishly.

"Well, look," I said. "It's no big deal. I really don't have time to be in a fraternity anyway. Thanks for telling me though."

"I'm really sorry," he said.

That was the first time I had experienced systemic racism in such an overt way, and it was very disturbing and hurtful. What I didn't know was that the Greek system of sororities and fraternities had been founded on the basis of White supremacy. Their charters denied access to Black, Brown and Jewish people. In doing the research for this book, I took out my old 1966 yearbook and turned to the pages that had the pictures of those in each organization. I was shocked to see that there was only one Spanish-surnamed person in any of them. (This in spite of the fact that the college was 60 percent Hispanic.) That person was Joe Gomez, a member of Tau Kappa Epsilon, TKE. Needless to say there were no black faces either. Strange that I had never noticed before. In a 2017 interview with Joe (who is Puerto Rican), he explained how he and his friend, Richie Mesa, had been rudely snubbed when they went through rush in the fall of 1965. However, they were the first to break the racial barrier when they were accepted by TKE. He explained that TKE "had been dormant, but was anxious to get new members and they weren't racist." TKE became a refuge for marginalized students, but then it was shunned by the other Greek organizations. While the other fraternities were having social events with sororities, no such thing was happening at TKE. "Being snubbed by Greek organizations was the second time I felt racism," Joe explained. "Once when I had a date with an Anglo girl, I arrived at her door to pick her up, only to have the door slammed in my face by her father who took one look at me and said 'My daughter's not going out with no spic.' I was forced to limit my dating to girls who lived in the dorms, because they were from out of town."

Amazingly, Joe was driven to overcome his adversity. Even though he worked 40 hours a week at the Fort Bliss Post Exchange, he was able to maintain a 3.8 grade-point average and he was voted president of the interfraternity council in 1967. In the spring of 1968, the faculty selected him as "the All-Greek Man" based on grades, activities and volunteerism. Among his many other achievements, Joe was named outstanding ex-student at Burges High School and he was inducted into the El Paso County Historical Society "Hall of Honors" for his community service.

But the upshot of my own experience in 1962 was that I became even more aware of racism all around me, not just against Mexicany people, but against other ethnicities as well. El Paso didn't have a very large percentage of African Americans at the time, so I hadn't observed the racist experiences they must have endured, but I was very aware that the Civil Rights Movement in the Deep South was picking up steam. Little did I know that a few years later the army would send me to Georgia and Southeast Alabama in the mid-1960s, just after passage of the Civil Rights Act. I would get a firsthand look at the incredibly hateful and violent racism that existed there as efforts to desegregate the South were in full swing.

(As an important side note, the Texas Western basketball team made history the year I graduated (1966) when they won the NCAA basketball tournament by fielding, for the first time ever, an all-black team, against the all-white University of Kentucky team. This was not because we had many black students, because, in fact, we had very few. It was because most of the best African-American players in the country were not being recruited by other schools. Our school got the cream of the crop because there was very little racism toward blacks at the time in El Paso. I was proud of our school for doing the right thing, but the national media, such as *Sport's Illustrated*, took the college to task for breaking the racial barrier. Texas Western not only broke the barrier, but it changed college sports forever after. Go Miners! The college became known for its stand against racism in sports. Funny that at the same time, its Greek organizations were (almost) completely segregated and, as far as I knew, no one said a thing.)

After my tour of duty in Vietnam, the army sent me back to Ft. Rucker,

Alabama, to complete the last few months of my three-year commitment. Because of my experience as a public information officer, I was assigned to be the assistant to the chief editor of the *U.S. Army Aviation Digest Magazine* and when my time was up, the editor asked me to stay on as a civilian, doing basically the same job. I left work on Friday afternoon as a captain in the army, and I returned on Monday morning in civilian clothes, as a civil service employee, one of the youngest GS-11s in the system. I had the same office and the same stack of papers on my desk. You could say it was one of the smoothest transitions ever from life in the military to civilian life. I would remain in that job for another year—plenty of time to get to know the locals and to have some serious discussions with them about racism.

In the office where I worked there were several local women who worked as secretaries and through them I learned to speak "Alabamish." One of my first days there, I asked one of them what her husband did for a living and she told me he was a "tar" salesman. I made a mental note to recommend him to anyone who needed a new roof. It was much later that I discovered that he didn't sell tar. What she was trying to say was that he was a "tire" salesman.

Another time the office workers were talking about how much they loved bald peanuts. I interjected that I had never heard of bald peanuts, perhaps because peanuts were not grown where I came from. I asked them to bring some to the office so I could try them, so they did. One of the ladies brought in a can labeled, "boiled peanuts." I made the grievous error of telling them they were not "bald" peanuts, because that would indicate the peanuts had no hair. I also made the mistake of correcting the other lady who pronounced the word "tire" as "tar." She was not appreciative. In fact, they accused me of being a "damned Yankee." I assured them I wasn't and told them I was from West Texas, but that had no effect on them. They accused me of speaking with a Yankee accent and having Yankee ideas.

When the discussion turned to the way Black people were treated in the South, one of them cut me off and said, "Look here. We don't want to talk about this anymore. As far as we're concerned, they're just animals."

As it turned out, this attitude toward African-Americans was not peculiar to the office girls; it seemed to be the common view. When I went to rent an apartment in a nearby town, I was asked by the owner a question that startled me. "Before you sign the lease, I have one more question," he said.

"Okay," I said. "What is it?"

"Is your wife White?" he asked. I was stunned. The Civil Rights Act specifically forbade landlords from discriminating on the basis of race, but that didn't stop him. His actions reminded me of something I studied in high school, but didn't take seriously: Manifest Destiny. It is the old idea that White Anglo-Saxons were a special race and rightfully the superiors of other peoples. This false notion gave them the liberty to force the native peoples from their lands and convert them to Christianity, even by force, if necessary. Unfortunately this notion is still shared today by many whites, and not only in the Deep South.

It was then I realized I had to get out of the South. I just couldn't take it anymore. Even the churches were segregated! Since the military had no more hold on me, I could go wherever I wished, as long as I could make a living, so I started looking at options. What came to mind immediately was graduate school. The G.I. Bill would pay me $300/month to continue my education for three years. I had already used up one year by completing a master's degree in education by attending night classes offered by Troy State University. I decided it was time to fulfill one of my dreams and to apply to the graduate school at the University of Missouri, School of Journalism. I was quite surprised to learn that my old TWC journalism professor, Dr. Ralph Lowenstein, the one who approved my story on the stripper, Georgia Storm, was now a professor there, and he remembered me. How could he not?

Dr. Lowenstein is and was a devout Jew who ran off to fight in the War of Independence for the State of Israel in 1948 when he was 18 years old, even though he was breaking U.S. law. Afterward, he wrote a book about his experience titled, *Bring my Sons from Far*. Prior to teaching at the University of Missouri, he was a professor of journalism at Tel Aviv University, and after leaving Missouri, he became the dean of the school of communication at the University of Florida, and is now Dean Emeritus. He was awarded the Emma Lazarus Statue of Liberty by the American Jewish Historical Society (their highest honor) for demonstrating outstanding leadership and commitment strengthening the American Jewish Community. I am proud to call him my good friend today in 2018.

However, in 1970, when I contacted him about applying to the Missouri graduate school, I wasn't sure what kind of response I would get, so I was a bit shocked when I reached him by phone and he immediately supported my idea.

"Look," he said, "I'll help you get a scholarship, in-state tuition, and the premier student job here at the J. school, but there is a catch."

"What's the catch?" I asked a bit apprehensively.

"You'll have to be enrolled in the Ph.D. program."

"But I don't want a Ph.D.," I complained. "I just want another master's degree. "I don't think I'm Ph.D. material."

"I know you. You can do it. Sign up for the Ph.D. program and I'll help you," he said encouragingly.

"Ok,ay" I said, "If you say so."

Two weeks later, I resigned my job in Alabama and I was on my way to Missouri. Dr. Lowenstein was true to his word. I received a scholarship to defray my moving expenses, I was approved for in-state tuition and I got the job as editor of the *Freedom of Information Digest and Reports*, published at the school of journalism. The job paid $300 per month for 20 hours a week, allowing me to carry a full load of courses, which kept the G.I. Bill money rolling in. What more could I have asked for? Lowenstein served as my advisor throughout the program.

The two years of course work passed quickly and much too soon I had to come up with an idea for a dissertation, and then sell the idea to my committee, made up of four Ph.D. professors, and the former editor of the

Chicago Daily News—a hardcore newsman who had recently been made dean of the school. After fishing about for a topic, I was finally drawn back to the issue of civil rights, so I proposed conducting a sociological study of the Mexican-American Civil Rights Movement, with emphasis on how this grass-roots movement was able to get its story out to the public through the mass media. The title was: "Uses of the Media by the Chicano Movement." The committee liked the idea and gave me a green light. Now I had to find someone to help fund my research, as I felt it would be necessary to spend a considerable amount of time in Washington, D.C.

After pondering this problem, I decided to use my imagination once again to find a solution. I imagined someone sitting at a desk in Washington, D.C., bored with his job, and anxious to meet with a young Ph.D. student who had an interesting project in mind. This person would have the resources to fund my project. There was only one thing to do; I would have to go to Washington and find him. So at spring break I bought an airplane ticket, made arrangements to sleep on a friend's couch for a few days and I went to Washington armed with a list of names and phone numbers I had compiled of those who might be helpful.

My first call the next day was to the offices of the Mexican-American Anti-Defamation Committee (MAADC), chaired by a fiery Mexican-American by the name of Domingo Nick Reyes. His organization had already found success in getting negative stereotypes of Mexicans taken off the air, such as Frito Lay's cartoon character, the "Frito Bandido." Reyes had lobbied Congress and organized national boycotts of products that used negative images of Mexicans in their advertisements. I thought he would be sympathetic to my research project, as it would include the impressive work he and his organization had done in this area.

I dialed the number and I quickly got Reyes on the phone.

"Hello, Mr. Reyes," I said. "My name is Joe Lewels and I am a Ph.D. student at the University of Missouri. I would like to drop by to meet you and interview you for research I'm doing for my doctoral dissertation."

"So how much are you going to pay me?" he asked.

"I don't understand," I replied. "I just want to speak to you for the research I'm doing. It's an academic project. I don't have money to pay you."

"All you Anglos ever want is to use us Mexicans for your own good. We're tired of being used. If you want to interview me you will have to pay," he said, rudely.

There was only one thing I could do at this point. I would have to work some magic. I would have to try to speak to him in Spanish. So, I said, "*Perdoneme Señor Reyes, pero yo también soy Mexicano. Mi nombre es Francisco Jose Lewels Cisneros.*" ("Excuse me Mr. Reyes, but I am also a Mexican, my name is Franciso Jose Lewels Cisneros.")

There was a long moment of silence at the end of the line, and then he said in perfect English, "Oh, that's different. Why didn't you say so in the first place? What time do you want to come over?"

"Well, how about now?" I said.

"Okay, sure. Come on over," he said, in a most courteous tone.

I had the distinct impression that Domingo Nick Reyes didn't speak Spanish, or if he did, it wasn't very good Spanish. He, after all, was from Denver, not from the border.

I found Nick, as he liked to be called, sharing an office with one other Mexicany guy. The highly-publicized and successful MAADC, I found, was a two-man office with sparse furnishing and no secretary. But Nick and his partner, Armando Rendón, couldn't have been nicer. By the end of my long interview with them, Nick insisted I go home with him so his wife, Conchita, could cook us up some good, home-made Mexican food. He wouldn't take no for an answer. That evening became crucial in my effort to find funding for my project. During dinner, Nick said, "You need to go see Gil Pompa at the Justice Department. He's the guy to see. I'll call him first thing tomorrow and make an appointment for you."

"Who is Gil Pompa?" I asked. "He's not on my list of people to call."

"Gil is the associate director of the Community Relations Service (CRS) at the Department of Justice (DOJ). He used to be the assistant district attorney for the city of San Antonio."

"I've never heard of the Community Relations Service," I said. "What does it do?"

"Don't feel bad, not many people know about the CRS; it tries to lay a low profile. It was created under Title X of the Civil Rights Act as an agency with the power to ensure that the Civil Rights act is implemented in five areas: education, law enforcement, housing, healthcare and communications. They have been working on helping Chicano groups gain access to the media. He will be interested in your project for sure," he said.

The next afternoon I was seated in front of Pompa, who had risen to become a high-level player in the Civil Rights Movement. He seemed pleased to have his busy day interrupted by someone with an interesting idea.

"Would you like a cup of coffee?" he asked me as I sat down.

"Yes, thank you," I replied. "Make mine black."

I spent about 15 minutes explaining who I was and what I was working on and then he asked me a series of questions.

"Are there any other Mexican-Americans working on Ph.D.s at Missouri?"

"No. I'm the only one."

"Are there any at other universities?"

"I don't know. Not that I'm aware of," I answered.

"How about master's degrees? Any Mexican-Americans at Missouri getting master's degrees?

"None that I know of," I answered.

"What about African Americans?"

"No, I don't know of any," I answered.

"Okay, then," he said in a decisive tone. "You're hired."

"Hired?" I asked in surprise. "No, I'm not looking for a job, I just need some funding for my research. I'll have to spend a lot of time here in Washington and traveling around the country."

"Yes, that's what I'm talking about," he said. "We'll hire you as a civil-service employee and we'll send you wherever you need to go. We'll open all our files to you and, with your Department of Justice credentials, you'll have access to the Federal Communications Commission (FCC) files or to any other government agency files you see fit. When you're finished with your dissertation and you get your degree, maybe you'll want to stay on with us as a communication specialist."

"Wow! That is very generous of you. But what do you want out of this?" I asked.

I want you to give full credit to the CRS in your dissertation and I want a copy of it when you're finished," he said.

"That's it?" I asked skeptically.

"That's it," he said. "Get the paperwork from my secretary. You can start as soon as the semester is over."

Before the end of May, 1972, I was ensconced in a small office in an office building on 11th street in Washington D.C., and for the next few months I traveled the country meeting with Community Action Groups (CAGs) which had sprung up to help implement the ideals of the Civil Rights Movement. It was their contention that the mass media consciously and unconsciously deny access to minority groups, thereby creating a monopoly on opinion and news. They cited the fact that local broadcast stations and newspapers discriminated against Mexican-Americans in their hiring practices and thus did not represent the views of this growing minority.

At first, these groups were unsophisticated in their approach. They began publishing their own, small-circulation newspapers and created inexpensive events to bring attention to their causes. In California, the movement led by César Chavez to aid the farmworkers, conducted mass marches which gained the media's attention. To make people aware of their strike against the grape growers, they stamped the words, "Don't buy grapes," on helium-filled balloons and handed them out to children as they were entering grocery stores with their mothers. This caused the grocery-store owners to instruct employees to take the balloons away from the kids, which, in turn, caused mothers to take their screaming kids out of the stores. It was simple, but effective.

As the movement grew, the CRS held conferences around the country where activist leaders could meet with public interest lawyers (many funded by the United Church of Christ) who would assist them in challenging the licenses of broadcast outlets in their home towns. Here is where the movement gained traction as it was federal law that broadcasters serve the public interest of all members of their communities. To ensure they did so, the FCC required all broadcasters to conduct surveys of members of their community and to provide local programming to meet their needs. These surveys were considered to be available to the public upon request. Broadcasters who failed to comply were in jeopardy of losing their very lucrative licenses.

There was a problem. Most people had no idea that there was such a requirement and, therefore, no one ever asked to see the surveys. As a result, broadcasters across the country had regularly faked the surveys. When the local activists and their lawyers asked to see the surveys, broadcast owners immediately capitulated to their demands. The effect was immediate and easily apparent. Minority faces began appearing on local newscasts and special programming, created by local activist groups, began being aired. The national movement to challenge the licenses of the owners of broadcast stations changed the face of television programming almost overnight. The print media were another thing altogether, as they face no federal requirement to serve the public interest. They only have to serve the interest of their shareholders.

I had been in Washington only about a month when I decided to walk over to the FCC offices to do some more research, as I had many times before. But this time I decided, on a whim, to take a slight detour down a small lane lined by charming old row houses. It was a hot summer afternoon, but I was enjoying the sights and in no particular hurry, as I had no boss and no set schedule. It was then that I spotted a brass plaque on the front of one of the row houses. It read, "Praeger Publishing Company." I stopped in front of the sign and contemplated its significance. I had heard of Praeger Publishing because it was a large New York firm, so I was only mildly surprised to see they had offices in Washington. That meant they were interested in publishing books about currents affairs. So, I walked in the front door and stood before the receptionist.

"I would like to talk to an editor," I boldly proclaimed.

"What about?" she asked.

"I am writing a book that Praeger might be interested in publishing," I responded.

"Well," she said, "let me see if anyone is available. Have a seat."

I sat in the waiting area for about five minutes before a tall, middle-age, lanky guy in a short-sleeve shirt and a tie came out through a door behind the receptionist's desk.

"Can I help you?" he asked as he extended his hand.

I stood up, took his hand and said, "I'm writing a book I think you will be interested in. Could I bother you for a few minutes so I can tell you about it?"

"Okay, come on back," he said.

He led me through the door and down a hall to his office, not much bigger than mine at the CRS. He had a stack of manuscripts on his desk. "Would you like a cup of coffee?" he asked.

"Sure," I said.

"Cream and sugar?" he asked.

"No thank you, just black," I answered.

After about a 20-minute conversation, which he seemed to enjoy, he said, "Well why don't you send me the first chapter of your book and a one-page summary of each additional chapter and I'll take that to the board of directors. Let's see what happens."

"Sure," I said. "I'll get it to you in a week or so."

As I was leaving he gave me his card. "Send it to my attention," he said.

It took me about two weeks to complete the first chapter and the summaries of the additional chapters. By then, the structure of the dissertation had been swimming in my head for some time. I put it in an envelope and sent it to his attention. About three weeks later, I received a large, manila envelope in the mail from Praeger Publishing Company. I quickly tore it open to find a contract for my book. They offered me a $5,000 advance. All I had to do was sign it and return it to them. It sounded too good to be true, so I called Dr. Lowenstein in Missouri to ask his advice.

"Dr. Lowenstein," I started, "Praeger Publishing Company has offered to publish my dissertation. They sent me a contract in the mail, but it's a long, legal document and I'm not sure if I should get a lawyer to look at it. Maybe I can send it to you to look at it."

"Sign it!" he said. "Just sign it and send it back."

"But I don't know anything about contracts," I pleaded. "I think I should have someone look at it first."

"You don't understand," he said. "In the entire history of the school of journalism since it opened in 1908, there has never been a dissertation that was published. Yours will be the first. Just sign the darned thing and send it back. Congratulations."

Needless to say, I signed the darned thing and sent it back. It took me another six months to complete the manuscript and by then I had returned to El Paso, as I needed a quiet place to organize the mountain of information I had collected. It was good to be home. I had deferred making a decision regarding my return to Washington as I was committed to completion of my degree. I had been warned that many Ph.D. candidates fail to graduate because they never complete their dissertations. That wasn't going to happen to me.

Shortly after returning home, I was asked to teach a course at my old college, which by then was known as the University of Texas at El Paso, or UTEP (Go Miners!). They gave me an office in a quiet part of the campus, and it was there that I typed into the long hours of the night in an effort to get the manuscript back to my committee in Missouri and to the publisher in Washington by the deadlines I was given.

It was in late 1973 that I drove back to Missouri for the oral defense of my dissertation which was by then completed. The oral defense gives the advisory committee a chance to nitpick, critique and attack the premise and the final product, and it is traditionally and historically one of the most stressful moments for a Ph.D. candidate. Somehow, I wasn't in the least bit worried. My manuscript had been accepted by the publisher and was in the process of being published and I knew there was no way they could give me a failing grade.

Normally, the oral exam lasts for an hour or even two, but mine lasted perhaps 30 minutes. The only thing they wanted to know was "How did you manage to get it published?" A couple of them had not published a book. They had never considered that a Ph.D. dissertation could ever be published. So, I told them about my stroll over to the FCC and how I saw a plaque on the wall and how I just went in and asked to see an editor.

"You just walked in without an appointment?" One asked skeptically.

"You mean you didn't even have a manuscript when you walked in?" another asked. They were taken aback.

The book was published in 1974 under the title: *Uses of the Media by the Chicano Movement: A Study in Minority Access*. The author was listed as Francisco J. Lewels, Jr. It was clear that things had changed and being identified as Mexicany had its advantages, thanks to the fact that the issue of Mexican civil rights was in the news.

Then, just before the book was published, the chairman of the UTEP journalism department suddenly died and I received a visit from the dean of liberal arts, who wanted to chat. He came right to the point. "We want you to be chairman of the department," he said.

I was shocked. "But I've only taught one course; I don't think I'm qualified for the job," I pleaded.

"You're the only one in the department with a Ph.D. and you've published a book as well as numerous journal articles. That's more than most of the faculty on the whole campus has done. You're going to do just fine," he argued.

"I don't know. I have a job waiting for me back in Washington and I was planning to go back when the semester ended. Besides, this journalism program is in really bad shape. We need more full-time people who have at least a master's degree, along with professional experience, and the whole curriculum is out of date," I complained.

"The president authorized me to offer you the position and to give you our full support. You'll be able to turn the program around," he said. "Of course, we'll have to drop by our new Chicano Studies Program to get their approval, but I wouldn't worry about that."

"Well, this has caught me by surprise, I need a few days to think it over," I responded. It seemed clear that the Mexican-American Civil Rights Movement had not only changed the face of broadcasting, but also the face of higher education. UTEP was under pressure to higher more Mexican-American professors and department chairmen. It seemed that my "Mexicanyness" was now working in my favor.

By the next day I realized another door had been opened by mysterious forces. I was being handed another amazing opportunity. Besides, the Mexican border had cast its spell on me once again. It was good to be back where people spoke Spanish or Spanglish, or whatever, and I loved being close to family. I called Washington and told them about my decision. I wouldn't be going back.

Very unexpectedly, I could see that El Paso had captured me in its powerful grasp—a grasp from which I would never be able to escape.

I was home, where I belonged.

21

Chapter *Veinte y Uno*
Ghosts and Other Weirdness

As in most cultures around the world, ghost stories loom large in Mexico; they are told and retold in most families, and mine was no exception.

A popular tale is about a woman called "La LLorona," (the weeping woman), which is often used to scare kids from going out at night. As the story goes (this is the abbreviated version), a beautiful young woman from a small village fantasizes about marrying a rich nobleman. One day a dashing young man on a fine stallion is riding by and, by chance, they meet and are later married and have two children. But eventually the man regrets having married a woman of a lower class and he leaves her and the children, never to return.

In a fit of jealous rage and grief, the woman throws her children into a fast flowing river, but instantly regrets her action and goes in after them. She and her children drown. After that night, people say they often hear the wailing of the woman by the river and see a ghostly figure walking on the riverbank in a long, flowing, white gown. "Don't go to the river at night," the parents tell their kids. "La llorona will get you."

However, there is a difference between ghost stories and stories about real ghost, like the ones that kept my family and extended family on edge. Here are a few I will share with you.

"They moved again," my mom told me with a troubled expression on her face one day as we were having lunch at her modest home in east El Paso. My dad had already passed and my mom lived alone, with a Mexican housekeeper named "Tere," (short for Teresa). Within a week of my dad's passing, my mom complained she couldn't live alone because she was afraid of the ghosts, so we (her three kids) chipped in and paid for a housekeeper to live with her. But Tere was the fifth or sixth maid to work there. None of them lasted very long. Each one had packed her bags hurriedly and fled without notice because of the ghosts. Some lasted only a few days, others a few weeks. It had been a virtual revolving door of housekeepers and every time one left we were left with the task of finding a new one. I didn't want the family to go through that process again.

"You mean the dolls?" I queried with a queasy feeling of frustration.

"Well, that's what she says."

"Do you think she's going to leave?" I asked nervously.

"I don't know. She's pretty tough, but that's all she talks about. Not just the dolls but the spirits that follow her around the house, and then there's the man at night," my mom explained.

The dolls we were talking about were old Mexican marionettes that my dad bought years before to entertain the grandkids, of which he had seven. One of the dolls bore the likeness of a Mexican boy, wearing a white shirt and pants, a red bandana around his neck and a sombrero on his head. The other was of a girl with long braids and colorful blouse and skirt. The strings that controlled the hands and feet had gotten hopelessly entangled years ago and had been cut off. Now they were just dolls. They had been an endless source of amusement for him and the grandkids for many years, so they held a lot of sentimental value for us, and still do.

When my dad passed, we placed the dolls on his desk, one seated on each end. Tere had claimed for some time that she would find them in different places, thus spooking her so much she would walk around the house mumbling prayers to herself. Tere was a large woman in her late forties, or so we thought. She had a broad face and shoulders and was much older than the ones who came before her. She didn't seem to be the type who would be intimidated easily, but she appeared to be in a state of constant nervousness.

"So have you ever seen the dolls move?" I asked my mom who was in her mid-80s and still maintained her faculties.

"No, I haven't. I don't think Tere has seen them move either," she explained. "They just appear in different places, or so she says."

Now you might think I didn't take any of this story seriously, but, as a matter fact, I did. It wasn't just because I didn't want the family to have to go through the difficulty of finding yet another companion for my mom—one we could trust to care for her, one she could get along with (no easy task) and one who wasn't afraid of a little-old ghost. There was another reason I had for taking the story seriously. That was because there had always been weird goings on in our house and in the home of some of my relatives in Mexico.

For example, there were the hauntings at our cousin's house in Chihuahua City—a house we used to visit when I was a kid. Because my uncle was a very successful surgeon and director of the medical school, the family occupied a sumptuous two-story home with a swimming pool in the back yard by the orchard. The white-stucco home had a red-tile roof and the Mexican-tile floors were so shiny I could slide on them in my socks. The whole place smelled of cedar wood and the high ceilings made it appear to me to be like a castle, compared to how we lived back home. My five cousins and their many friends, running in and out of the many rooms always created an air of great expectation and excitement for me, though I was only four or five when I first remember visiting.

We all looked forward to our visits, even though we knew there were ghosts around. It was a known fact. Our cousins had filled us in on the history of the place on our first visit. It seems that the property on which the home was built was reputed to have had a ghostly light, eerily roaming the spacious grounds at night. All the neighbors said so. But undeterred, my skeptical uncle went ahead and built the house on the haunted land.

From the beginning, after moving in, the family began hearing strange noises, day and night. There were footsteps heard in places where no one had been. There was the ball that bounced up and down the stairs at night. One night, we were told, some of the kids were playing in the back yard, but they ran into the kitchen for a glass of water. They were stopped dead in their tracks when they saw a fly swatter floating in midair in the middle of the kitchen. Then, it flew across the room and clattered onto the floor, causing them to turn and flee the house, shrieking and screaming in horror.

One of my male cousins told us about the time he was asleep in his bed when he felt a hand grasp his arm firmly and begin trying to pull him out of his bed. The most frightening part of the story was that his bed was pushed up against a wall and the hand came out of the wall to get him. "What did you do?" I asked, seriously spooked.

"I just moved away from the wall and pulled the covers over my head," he said. Even though the hand never returned, the story kept me awake at night and away from the walls.

One afternoon, my sister Helen found herself alone in the house and heard footsteps coming up the stairs and toward the back bedroom where she was napping. She called out to ask who it was, but there was no answer. It scared her so badly that she ran to the bathroom and locked herself in until everyone got home. Stories like these were so common that it seemed the family had just become accustomed to having a family ghost.

And then there were the ghosts at our home—a house we moved into when I was seven and where my mom lived after my dad died. Both my sister and my brother, David, claimed to have seen a dark figure of a man standing in the hallway near their bedrooms at night and at different times. My mom had also seen a man standing in her bedroom at night on more than one occasion. When she told me that story I asked her skeptically, "So mom, if you saw a man standing in your room at night, why didn't you get up and call the police?"

"I don't know," she answered sheepishly. "I just went back to sleep. But that's not the only thing that happened," she continued. "One day all the books on the bookshelf in my room just flew out onto the floor, right before my eyes!" she exclaimed excitedly.

It seemed that only my dad and I had never witnessed any ghost activity, which should have made us skeptical of such claims, but I never pushed my mom too hard on the ghost stories because it had already been proven to me that my mom's paranormal experiences were real. I saw it for myself on several occasions. For example, there was the time my sister went to visit a friend in Phoenix and my mom worried about her being away from home for the first time. One morning while my sister was away, my mom was very excited at breakfast. "I was there last night!" she exclaimed!

"What are you talking about?" my dad asked.

"It was like a dream, but it was too real to be a dream. I really went to the house where Helen is staying. It's a small yellow house with a white picket fence around it. I walked up to the front door and almost went in, but I knew I shouldn't, so I came back into my body."

She was so excited, she ran to her room and retrieved a pencil and a sheet of paper and began to draw the house in great detail. She drew a house with a front gate and a walkway up to the front door. The gate was ajar and a garden hose crossed the walkway, halfway up to the house; there was a sprinkler attached at the end.

"That's crazy," my dad said in his usual skeptical way. But I trusted my mom implicitly and held back my pronouncement until after my sister returned and either confirmed or debunked my mother's story. A few days later when she returned, my mother began to question her about the house she had seen in her "dream." My sister was amazed at the accuracy of my mom's description. Then she remembered that she had a photo of the house and she quickly ran to her room to fetch it. She laid it down on the dining room table and my mom retrieved her sketch and laid it down next to the picture. We all crowded around to see what the evidence showed. Even my dad was dumbfounded by the similarities. The two were identical in every way, even the open gate and the garden hose draped across the walkway. It was hard for me to conclude anything other than my mother's spirit had somehow traveled to Phoenix to check on her daughter that night.

Another time, when I had gone to California after high school, I decided to return to El Paso on the spur of the moment, without telling anyone. I caught a ride with a friend who was leaving within the hour, so I packed my bag and we were off. It was around three a.m. when he dropped me off in front of my house, so I expected to see the house darkened and everyone asleep. To my surprise, I noticed the light in my mom's bedroom was on, and even more surprising was that she was sitting at the window, which faced the front driveway. It was as if she was waiting for me. When I walked in the door she ran up and threw her arms around me in a big hug. "Mi Rey," she said, "I'm so glad you're home safely. I have been so worried."

"What are you doing up? I said. "You should be asleep at this hour."

"I don't know," she answered. "I just had a strange feeling that I needed to get out of bed and get dressed. I even put on my makeup and combed my hair. Then I just sat in my chair by the window and waited. But I didn't know for what—until you drove up."

After a few moments of trying to process this strange event, I finally said, "Well, you can go back to bed now. It's late and I'm okay. We can talk about it in the morning." But I already understood what happened. I knew that my mom and I had a special connection and that somehow, telepathically, some part of her knew I would be arriving. Yes, my sweet, little, unsophisticated mom had extrasensory perception (ESP); I had seen too many examples of her abilities over the years to question it any longer, so I just went to bed and promptly fell asleep.

But the issue before me now was not my mom, it was the problem of the dolls, and I needed to get to the bottom of the story by having a little chat with the housekeeper, Tere, a chore I was not looking forward to because once you got her going in a conversation it was near impossible to get her to stop talking. She was like a prisoner who had been in isolation for years and couldn't wait to have someone's ear. But as much as she talked, she was never too forthcoming about her life. We knew very little about her, other than that she was from Mexico, as they all were, and that she had no children and was not married. She had kept my mom entertained and occupied for more than two years. That was enough for us.

Tere said she was from Juárez, but her demeanor and mannerisms gave the impression of someone who had grown up on a ranch or in a small village. In all probability, she was undocumented. We never asked and we didn't care; she needed the work and we needed the help. And my mom had very limited resources.

Although my sister was the primary caregiver, due to the fact that she lived closest to her, and she was the oldest of the three siblings, I would drive across town every Friday to have lunch and to check in on her. It seemed to be always the highlight of her week and we would spend an hour or so chatting about anything she wanted to talk about. Tere would prepare the same delicious meal every time—a chicken broth soup with vegetables and refried beans on the side, served with a flower tortilla and sliced avocado. The menu never varied.

After serving the meal, she would linger in the background, listening in on our conversation, so we spoke in English to keep her from jumping in to make a point that would take at least 10 minutes. She was dying to be a part of the conversation, so on this particular day, I decided to let her in and I began by addressing her in Spanish and complementing her on her cooking.

At once, her broad face lit up, her extra-large and very white teeth stood out in contrast to her dark-brown skin, and her high cheekbones were raised even higher by her big smile. "Oh, thank you, señor," she said in great anticipation.

"Tere, my mother says that the dolls moved again. Can you tell me what happened?"

"Oh yes, they did move again," she said, her face suddenly going from a big smile to an expression of great concern. "You know there are spirits in this house and they like to play games by moving the dolls around. I always put them in their places, but in a day or so, when I go in to dust your father's room, they have changed places. Sometimes I find them on a shelf or on top of the dresser. Many times I can feel someone standing behind me or at my side, but when I turn, there is no one there."

"Well," I said trying to make light of the situation, "it all seems quite harmless. I don't think you are in any danger do you?"

"No senor, you are correct. I know my prayers to our Father and to His son, Jesus, protects me from harm, but I still don't like it," she said as she made the sign of the cross with her right hand.

"Okay, that's good," I with a bit of relief. "Would it make you feel better if I took the dolls home with me?" I asked. "Maybe that would help you to feel safer."

"Oh yes señor, thank you, thank you. That is a very good idea."

"Very well then," I said firmly, trying to bring the discussion to a quick end. "I'll take them with me today."

"But señor," she went on. "There is one more thing I need to tell you and the señora. You see, my sister, who lives in California is ill and I must go to be with her for a month or so. I also have to go to the social security office in Juárez to straighten out problems with my pension payments. I must leave tomorrow, but I will most assuredly return. In the meantime I have arranged for a friend of mine to replace me while I am gone."

So that was that. Tere packed her bags and left us in a lurch the following day. True to her word, Tere's replacement showed up the next day and a month later Tere showed up at the door. My mom welcomed her back, glad to have the caregiver she had become so comfortable with for so long, but then Tere dropped another bombshell. "No senora," she said, "I am not Tere; I am her sister Nafrít. Tere told me all about you and your family and, if it pleases you, I will continue working for you in her place, just as Tere did before."

Of course, my mom was taken aback, as she could detect no difference between this new woman, Nafrít, and her old housekeeper, Tere. Nevertheless, she invited the newcomer in and went along with what she considered to be a strange turn of events.

That Friday, I arrived for lunch expecting to see the replacement maid, but instead, I found Tere serving lunch. When she saw me, she introduced herself as if we had never met and went through a complex story about how her sister, Tere, had broken her leg while in California and had asked her to take her place as my mother's caregiver. I was speechless. I could detect no difference between this woman and the one who had left a month before. Furthermore, the lunch she served that day was precisely the same as the lunch I had been served every week for two years.

Finally, I had to ask, "Nafrít," you look so much like Tere, that I assume you are twins." But instead of taking this opening to make her story more believable, she laughed loudly as if that were the silliest thing anyone had ever said to her.

"Oh no, senor, Tere is much older than I am; we are nothing alike."

I just stared at her with an expression of disbelief. I wasn't buying her story; I didn't believe it for a second. As far as I could tell, this woman was Tere, and yet I didn't want to rock the boat if my mom was happy with the situation. As soon as she was out of the room, I whispered to my mom: "Is she really the sister?" My mom just rolled her eyes and shrugged her shoulders. It was clear she wasn't buying the story either.

So here was the dilemma, either she was the same person and she was crazy or she was perpetrating some kind of fraud, possibly having to do with her social security payments. Perhaps she had stolen someone's identity in order to receive the woman's checks. If so, she was a criminal and shouldn't be trusted. In either case, we had to consider if it was appropriate for her to be taking care of our dear little mom. I decided to wait until I could sit down with my sister and have a serious discussion. For the moment, it seemed my mom was ok with Tere/Nafrít living with her, and good help was hard to find.

It was several weeks later when I had the opportunity to sit down with my sister and have a quiet conversation about the problem. We had not discussed the issue, even by phone. After some small talk, I came right to the point. "Is mom's housekeeper crazy or is she really a different person?"

Helen's eyes widened and her lips pursed, revealing this was not the first time she had thought about it. Finally, she said, "I don't know, what do you think?"

"I think she's the same person." I said.

"Yeah, I think you're right. What should we do?"

"Well, can we let Mom live with a crazy person or a crook?" I asked.

"I don't know," she answered. "Mom seems happy enough and there isn't anything of value in the house that could be stolen. Mom's social security checks go straight to her bank account that we control. I don't think she's dangerous. Mom just keeps calling her "Tere," no matter how many times "Nafrít" tries to correct her, so it's as if nothing has changed."

I thought that last comment was very funny as I believed Tere/Nafrít would never win that argument. My mom could be a bit stubborn at times and her ability to learn new names was not what it used to be. "So do we leave well enough alone?" I asked.

"Yeah," my sister answered, "I guess so. We might as well leave well enough alone and go along with her story. After all, good help is hard to find."

22

Chapter *Veinte y Dos*
"Who's In Charge Here?"

Often I have had to ask myself, "Who the heck is in charge here, anyway? Who's pulling my strings? Am I just a lucky guy (maybe extraordinarily lucky), or is there something else going on?"

Looking back on my life I noticed the many strange things I have witnessed and the many amazing coincidences there have been in which doors (or holes) just seemed to open up for me, almost as if there was some kind of conspiracy moving me along through life toward some predetermined goal. It seems to me they were teaching points provided by an invisible teacher to help me understand the true, hidden nature of reality.

Maybe I'm not as clever as I once thought when I was "gaming the system." Maybe these great ideas were put in my head by my teachers and I only believed they were my own. I have had to seriously consider the following questions: Is it possible that we live in a purposeful universe, rather than an accidental one? Are coincidences really just accidental or is there something else going on? The "smarter" I've gotten the more I have concluded there are no coincidences. Maybe figuring that out is what "getting smart" is all about. Maybe I'm not really in charge.

But if I am not in charge, and someone else is, then to what end have all these amazing things happened to me? What's the point? Perhaps my entire life has been orchestrated so that I could write this book about my efforts to get smart and about the many lessons I have learned. Maybe I am supposed to share these stories with you. Although I am still in the process of getting smart, here are a few things I can share with you, and maybe in the process you can think of how your own life has been guided by an unseen director who ultimately brought you to my book.

Lesson number one is that all things are connected, and at some very subtle level of reality we are all one. This is not just some new-age prattle; it is fact. Physicists have discovered that at the root of the material world, the quantum level of photons, electrons and other sub-atomic particles, everything is connected. Oneness is the primary characteristic of the universe we live in. Microbiologists studying the DNA molecule from which all life on earth springs, have discovered there is virtually no difference between the DNA of one human and that of another. Of course there are variances, but we all have the same number of letters in our DNA code. Scientists looking into the origins of life and of the universe have found that you, I, and all living things are all made of stardust. So why then is there so much racial strife in the world when we now know absolutely that we are all the same?

The reason of course is that we perceive, falsely, through our five senses, that there are differences. But our five senses are totally inadequate for discovering the true nature of the reality we live in. After all, there was a time when it was commonly believed that the earth was flat and that the sun revolved around earth, not the other way around. These false notions were due to the fact that our five senses just let us down. The way we perceive the world around us is not always the way it really is.

Lesson number two is that getting smart is all about being able to see beyond the obvious and to get past the fictional reality our senses are showing us. This is important because our behavior is informed by our perceptions and beliefs. In other words, if we believe that everyone and everything around us is separate from ourselves, then we will not see that doing harm to others, even the earth, is doing harm to ourselves. Living by the saying "What goes around, comes around," is a good philosophy. Another way of saying this is that there are consequences for our actions, both good and bad, but maybe not immediately. Maybe the consequences happen after we die.

Lesson three is that any form of racism or other form of egotistical behavior is wrong and will bring eventual consequences. Although my experiences with racism have not been as harsh as those of many other people of different races or ethnicities, I was given a ringside seat to observe how racism manifests itself in different places around the world. Beginning with my need to overcome my own racial barriers as a kid, I learned that how people perceived me on the outside was not who I really was on the inside. I knew I was Mexicany and I was okay with that, but it wasn't always okay with others. When I was about eleven years old, a little Anglo girl who lived in my neighborhood called me a "half breed." I had to go home and ask my mom what that meant. "Well," she said, "a half breed is someone who is part one thing and part another."

"Am I a half breed?" I asked.

"No, that's silly," she said. "You're not a half breed. Where did you hear such a thing?"

"This little girl down the street called me that," I said.

"Well, don't listen to her. She is just stupid and doesn't know what she's talking about."

"Oh, okay," I answered, and I let it go.

I wasn't particularly hurt or concerned by the girl's remark, after all, she was just a little girl, maybe eight years old. But it did make me wonder where she got the idea that I was a half breed. I didn't even know her. I had never seen her before. I thought, perhaps, her parents had told her that, and she was merely repeating what they said. However, I didn't know her parents and I doubted they knew my family. Maybe there was a rumor going around the neighborhood among the Anglo families. Maybe they were talking about which of their neighbors were Mexicany so as to keep their kids away from those kids. I never discovered the answer.

Looking back on it though I can see that back in the 1950s, when that incident occurred, there were undercurrents of racism in my neighborhood and the kids were picking up on their parent's racist notions. Over the years I have learned that is exactly how racism spreads: from parent to child. Lesson four is that racism has to be learned; it doesn't come naturally. Kids pick up on everything their parents say, both good and bad. And then they accept those beliefs as being true. Even worse, it is very hard for kids to break away from those beliefs as they grow older, so they pass it on to their kids as well.

Another way people learn to be racist is through the mass media. The television and motion picture industries have been traditionally controlled by a white/Anglo majority and the programing and content they provide reflect their views. The owners of the media simply hire others like themselves, which means there are very few minority writers, directors, actors, reporters and editors. How can the media possibly understand and reflect the problems and political issues that are pertinent to the lives of those who are not like themselves? Lesson five is that minority groups are typically portrayed by the media in stereotypical roles that are degrading and insulting. Of course that has changed a lot in the past 50 years, but in the 2016 Academy Awards, for example, members of minority groups were completely ignored. Why? Because, as it turns out, 95 percent of the members of the academy, who decide who receives a nomination are white/Anglos. This, in spite of all the work done by activist groups during the Civil Rights Movement of the 1960s and1970s.

When I was in Washington, D.C., working at the Department of Justice in the early 1970s, there was a television show called "The Jose Jiménez Show," starring a non-Mexicany actor named Bill Dana. He portrayed a dumb Mexican who spoke English with a bad Mexican accent and who worked in a menial job. The entire premise of the show was to degrade and make fun of a Mexican minority, which had no voice in media affairs. This show was finally cancelled when my friend, Domingo Nick Reyes, director of the Mexican-American Anti-Defamation Committee, mentioned in an earlier chapter, made an issue of it before Congress and asked Mexican-Americans to boycott the show's sponsors.

Many people (even some Mexican-Americans) asked what was so wrong with Jose Jiménez and the Frito Bandido? These characters were funny and even cute. But stereotyping of minorities has its inherent dangers. By demonizing or belittling people of color, those with foreign accents, or any minority, the media perpetuate racism in society and make bigotry acceptable behavior for the majority. Fortunately, the Civil Rights Movement did much to change the way the media portray minorities but it couldn't stop the media from giving copious air time to public officials who spout hateful, racist rhetoric. How can the little guy get that kind of publicity?

To get attention for the shameful living conditions and pay scale of Mexican laborers in the fertile fields of California, César Chavez, an organizer of the United Farm Workers Union, first led long marches to attract media attention to their cause. Then, he almost died during a twenty-five day hunger strike, in which thousands of farm workers led nightly vigils and prayers. This drew the attention of the national media and politicians. The grape growers and land owners countered by spending millions in advertising, which condemned the union efforts. This is a good example of how access to the media comes easily to the rich, but is hard fought for by the poor. Too often, minority groups feel so disenfranchised they resort to rioting to get their message of helplessness across.

While doing research on my own family history, I discovered some unsettling information regarding how refugees were treated upon their arrival to El Paso in the early days of the Revolution. One day at a mass held at St. Patrick's Cathedral, the priest told the Mexicans to vacate the Anglo-only temple and to go among their own kind. The wealthier leaders of the immigrant community complained to the bishop, but the bishop stood up for his priest. He pointed out that the poorer, dark-skinned Mexicans should go to another church on the south side of town where sermons were in Spanish.

Immigrant families were also complaining that St. Patrick's school was not accepting their children. Mexican parents seeking to enroll their children were asked to bring them in for an "interview." According to Dr. Victor Macias-Gonzalez's report titled, "The Exile of the Chihuahuan Upper Classes in El Paso, 1913-1930," published in the El Paso County Historical Society newsletter, "Password," in the winter of 2000 (vol. 45 #4), the "interview" was for the purpose of determining if the child's complexion was light enough to meet school requirements. "Children darker than a brown paper bag were refused admittance." The resulting protest was the beginning of civic action and the organization of the immigrant community. Ultimately, they created their own parish and constructed their own church and school in Sunset Heights. It was called "*La Sagrada Familia*" (or "The Holy Family"). This is where my family attended mass when I was a child and where my parents were married. But by the time my wife and I were married in 1974, the social norms had, thankfully, changed. We were allowed to wed at St. Patrick's Cathedral.

Lesson six is that immigrants (documented or not) are mostly good, hard-working people and America needs them. They don't come here to commit crimes, but to find work and to get away from the violence in their homeland. Along the border, most people and businesses have compassion for immigrants because they understand their plight. They hire Mexican workers without much regard for citizenship. It's our tradition. Without exception, whether it is to landscape your yard, to build your house, to clean your floors, or to flip your burgers, they are the hardest workers. They do the hard, dirty jobs with good humor, and they are grateful for the opportunity. We must find ways to give these good people a pathway to citizenship. Sure, they may not speak English at first, but their children will, if given a

La Sagrada Familia (Holy Family) Catholic Church still stands in Sunset Heights

chance. With each generation, they will become a little less Mexican and a little more Mexicany. I guarantee that most will become proud Americans and they will serve their country with honor. As for the criminals, they should be prosecuted just like anyone else.

America is getting old and Americans aren't having enough children. We need new, young workers to enter into the workforce, to pay taxes and inject money into the social security system. We need immigrants and we need to treat them with kindness and compassion, not with bigotry and racist rhetoric that some politicians find beneficial to their own selfish purposes.

Lesson seven is about standing up against racism and bigotry and not sitting back quietly when you see them in your daily life. In the example above regarding darker-skinned, poorer, Mexicans not being allowed to worship at St. Patrick's Cathedral, it was the wealthy, lighter-skinned Mexicans who stood up and used their status to complain to the bishop and it was they who organized the effort to build another church where all would be welcomed.

In my own life, I have learned that lesson well. I don't put up with racist comments that are made in a hurtful way. I have tried to stand up and speak for the underprivileged in my writing and in my teaching and lecturing. But the best examples I have had of people standing up for me when they could have done otherwise happened when I was in college at TWC in El Paso. First there was my professor, Dr. Ralph Lowenstein, who encouraged me to become a journalist and who was instrumental in helping me enroll in and complete the Ph.D. program at the University of Missouri.

The other person is someone I have written a lot about already in this book. You may have wondered why my friend, Gary Miller, was so important in my life, so I will tell you. As you may recall, some of my friends were encouraged to go through rush, and to pledge a fraternity. Gary was one of the small group of my friends who went through rush together. He and I had decided that we were only interested in one fraternity, Kappa Sigma. When the bids came out, I went by myself to pick up my envelope, which I found empty. A few days later I found out that I had been black-balled because of my Mexicanyness. What I found out later was that Gary had received a bid. He had the opportunity to be in a fraternity and enjoy the parties and meet sorority girls. But when he found out why I had been turned down, he quietly declined the offer.

When I told him he didn't have to that, he said, "Oh heck, we don't need those guys to have a good time, we can do fine by ourselves." If ever there was a person you would think might have had racist tendencies it would be someone who grew up in a small Texas town where racism was overt at the time, but Gary wasn't like that. Somehow, he had gotten smart somewhere along the way. He got it. That's what I call a stand-up guy, the kind of friend that comes along only once in a lifetime.

Finally, I recently discovered via DNA testing, that I am 77 percent European and 13.2 percent Native-American (meaning I am part Mayan or Aztec or one of the many indigenous tribes of Mexico.) That doesn't seem like much, but it is enough to have had a huge impact on my life, and for that I am grateful. That small percentage of Indian blood gave me the opportunity to feel what it was like to be marginalized by being discriminated against. That is a valuable lesson all people should experience. It gave me empathy for and a feeling of comradeship with people of color and the underprivileged. It made me want to fight for minority rights and to stand up for the "little guy." In short, it made me a better person. For that, I say, *Viva Mexico* and *Viva America*; we should not let petty differences get in the way of being good neighbors and friends.

ON the RIO GRANDE

References

Acosta, Ray Steve. *Revolutionary Days: A Chronology of the Mexican Revolution*. Albuquerque, NM: Editorial Mazatlan, 2010.

Gonzalez, Michael J. *The Mexican Revolution 1910-1940*. Albuquerque, NM: University of New Mexico Press, 2002.

Guzmán, Luis Martín. *Memoirs of Pancho Villa* (translated by Virginia H. Taylor). Austin, TX: University of Texas Press, 1965.

Lewels, Francisco J. *Uses of the Media by the Chicano Movement: A Study in Minority Access*. New York: Praeger Publishing, 1974.

Macias-Gonzalez, Victor, Ph.D. *The Exile of the Chihuahuan Upper Classes in El Paso, 1913-1930*. El Paso, TX: *Password: Journal of the El Paso County Historical Society*. Vol. 45, #4. Winter, 2000, pp. 175-195.

Meyer, Jean. *The Cristero Rebellion: The Mexican People Between Church and State*. London: Cambridge University Press, 1976.

Romo, David Dorado. *Ringside Seat to a Revolution: An Underground Cultural History of El Paso and Juarez 1893-1923*. El Paso, TX: Cinco Puntos Press, 2005.

Rosenberg, Alyssa. "The Long, Fraught Racial History of American Fraternities." *The Washington Post*, March 11, 2015.

Salinger, Pierre. *With Kennedy*. Garden City, N.Y.: Doubleday and Co. Inc., 1966.

Worthington, Patricia Heasly. *El Paso and the Mexican Revolution*. Charleston, S.C.: Arcadia Publishing, 2010.

About the Author

Joe Lewels is the author of *Uses of the Media by the Chicano Movement: A Study in Minority Access*; *The God Hypothesis: Extraterrestrial Life and its Implications for Science and Religion*; *Rulers of the Earth: Secrets of the Sons of God*; and numerous newspaper, magazine and journal articles.

He holds a Ph.D. in journalism and mass communication from the University of Missouri, an M.S. in education from Troy State University, and a B.A. in journalism from Texas Western College, now the University of Texas at El Paso (UTEP.) He was an associate professor with tenure and chairman of the departments of journalism and mass communication at UTEP from 1972-1982, and he was a vice president and an international financial advisor at Merrill Lynch from 1982-2013. He was the editor of the "Freedom of Information Digest" at the University of Missouri and a writer/editor at the "U.S. Army Aviation Digest Magazine" at Fort Rucker, AL.

He served as a communications consultant at the U.S. Department of Justice and at the Federal Communications Commission in 1972. During the war in the Republic of South Vietnam in 1967-68, he served in the U.S. Army as a reconnaissance pilot and public information officer for the 17th Combat Aviation Group. He was awarded the Bronze Star and Air Medal with oak leaf clusters for his service in combat.

To order additional copies of this book,
please send full amount plus $6.00 for
postage and handling for the first book and
$1.00 for each additional book.

Send orders to:

Galde Press, Inc.
PO Box 774
Hendersonville NC 28793

Visit our website at *www.galdepress.com*
and download our free catalog,
or write for our catalog.

ON the RIO GRANDE

Made in the USA
Columbia, SC
30 May 2018